Python Machine Learning

*A Deep Dive Into Python Machine Learning
and Deep Learning, Using Tensor Flow And
Keras: From Beginner To Advance*

Leonard Eddison

TABLE OF CONTENTS

INTRODUCTION

Throughout the recent years, artificial intelligence and machine learning have made some enormous, significant strides in terms of universal, global applicability. The ability to now be able to apply such algorithms via traditional and new dynamic programming languages allows us to interpret and understand these approaches much more eloquently. While machine and deep learning algorithms have become a common measure for significant model performance across multiple industries, the primary focus of this book will be to better understand how such algorithms are being applied specifically via financial markets through the usage of the python programming language. A language that continues to gain fast ground on other languages, due to its powerful versatility and adaptability to various types of APIs and platforms. This book is catered more towards someone who has already developed a relatively profound understanding with the python programming language, and is now looking to apply this skill set specifically towards machine and deep learning in finance. Throughout the book, we will outline a couple detailed scenarios in which we will apply different types of machine and deep learning algorithms towards real-life, financial market scenarios to help best bridge the connection between python and how it is being utilized in today's day and age when it comes to artificial intelligence in the financial landscape.

WHY MACHINE LEARNING?

The obvious question many will ponder when it comes to artificial intelligence and its applicability towards financial markets is, why even trust it? To answer such a question seems very complicated on the surface; in that at the end of the day, can traditional fund managers really trust something that essentially will make its decisions on its own in absence of human intervention? The ability to even fathom such an approach for many modern age fund managers is undoubtedly questionable, and risky. Despite such concerns, many managers are now actually implementing a hybrid type of system, in which they are warming up to the idea of applying machine learning to their managed portfolios. However, by doing so in a sense of more security, where they allow some brief sense of human intervention during times of elevated market volatility. Or rather, during moments in which the algorithms seem to be acting up and disregarding the evolving dynamics of the market.

Such an approach, while it does utilize artificial intelligence, may sure be critiqued by true Wall Street quants, in that it is not purely quantitative trading. Nonetheless, we will approach the concepts and algorithms for this book from a perspective that is designed entirely towards applying the fundamentals of pure artificial intelligence in different types of financial markets; one with no pure form of human, or hybrid, intervention whatsoever. The underlying reasoning being that at the end of the day, if we can seem to create powerful machine learning models to predict market performance on such a level, we can maybe begin to slowly strip the general notion of emotional and irrational investment decision making from the equation. Such decision making that has historically been proven to fail the investment philosophy for both retail and experienced fund managers in that during times of high market stress and turmoil. In short, such irrational decisions have been proven to have a higher probability of playing into many lackluster investment choices. And generally speaking, result in poor investment outcomes.

This is something pure artificial intelligence and machine learning attempt to resolve by completely stripping such emotional decision making, and letting the machine make the ultimate, most rational of decisions with the highest probability of profitability potential. And with that, let's jump into it! We will outline specifically a couple types of machine and deep learning algorithms that are beginning to be commonly used in the financial world for both retail traders, and large hedge fund managers. These algorithms being logistical regression, and recurrent neural networks. As you will notice, while the fundamental logic behind these algorithms are somewhat paralleled in reasoning, the mathematical mechanics that give way to their respective decision making process can significantly differ. For our first algorithm, we will be applying python's module, scikit-learn, for machine learning prediction and trading. Further information on this library can be obtained at:

http://scikit-learn.org/stable/

APPLYING LOGISTIC REGRESSION TO U.S. EQUITY MARKETS FOR PREDICTIVE TRADING (AMZN)

In our first algorithm example, we will be applying an approach called logistic regression to help us predict price movements for traditional stocks within the U.S. equity markets via python. Logistic regression is a mathematical approach that has been around for quite some time now with the fundamental understanding behind it serving as a form of predictive analysis, in which the dependent variable (y variable) is binary. Generally speaking, the dependent variable should be dichotomous in nature, with the absence of outliers. We should also be able to exhibit no multicollinearity, in which there should be no elevated correlations among the predictors (our x variables, or our features). From a mathematical perspective, logistic regression estimates a multiple learning regression function defined as:

$$\text{logit}(p) = \log\left(\frac{P(y=1)}{1-(p=1)}\right) = \beta_0 + \beta_1 x_{i1} + \beta_2 \cdot x_{i2} + \dots + \beta_p \cdot x_{im}$$

for $i = 1 \dots n$.

9

One careful thing to be very cognizant of for logistic regression, and for all machine learning algorithms for the most part, is the notion of overfitting. The thought behind this is that by adding independent variables to a logistic regression model, we will undoubtedly tend to increase the total variance explained in the predictor variable. Nonetheless, adding too many variables to our model can result in overfitting; something that can reduce the general foundation of the model beyond the data that we use to fit the model. In essence, providing us with false interpretations on how well our model fits the data in question. With that said, let's apply our mathematical foundation for logistic regression to the U.S. equity markets via python. For our specific example, we will use logistic regression to help us predict price movements for Amazon, Inc. (ticker: AMZN) one of the most valued and respected technology companies on Wall Street for many years now. For all purposes and intentions on our algorithms throughout the book, we will be using python version 3.6, and Pycharm, a very popular editor/compiler for python that allows us to run our code and generate output results. Pycharm can be downloaded at:

https://www.jetbrains.com/pycharm/

Please note that the full functioning code for all of our given examples will be included as attachments to the book as well. Upon downloading Pycharm, one can open up a new project, which will allow for a new .py, python file. We will first need to install all of the required libraries, or modules, our algorithm will need to run on. These are listed at the top of our code, and look like the following:

```python
import numpy as np
import pandas as pd
import matplotlib.pyplot as plt
import ffn
from pandas_datareader import data as pdr
import fix_yahoo_finance as yf
import datetime
yf.pdr_override()
```

Before attempting to write any code, please make sure that these modules have all been properly installed and linked to your project directory via Pycharm. These can best be installed generally by using Pycharm's very own internal capabilities to do so within the editor. Further, specific details on the install can be found at:

https://www.jetbrains.com/help/pycharm/installing-uninstalling-and-upgrading-packages.html

Upon successfully installing the libraries shown above, we will need to define a simple classification function; which will allow our algorithm to classify between buy and sell signals. The following function will return a 1 if the signal for the price movement on the stock is to be a buy and a -1 if the signal on the price movement on the stock is to be a sell. The classification function is displayed as the following:

```
def computeClassification(actual):
    if (actual > 0):
        return 1
    else:
        return -1
```

The 1 and -1 values that output from out classification function will be a result of Amazon's experienced daily stock returns. With that, we are now ready to import our data, which will be done via the yahoo_finance library we have installed and imported in. We must first designate a start and end date for our logistic regression, machine learning algorithm to run off. For our examples, we will span our start and end dates from January 1, 2010 through October 29, 2018, in the following manner:

```
start = datetime.datetime(2010,1,1)
end = datetime.datetime(2018,10,29)

df = pdr.get_data_yahoo('AMZN', start=start,
end=end)
```

Simply put, we are asking yahoo_finance to extract data for the ticker, AMZN, for our desired period of time, and assign it to the variable name 'df.' This will subsequently store the data in a newly created data frame by employing python's pandas module. From here, manipulating of the data will become much easier. The next step will be to calculate daily returns for AMZN. We will be using the daily close price from our pandas data frame 'df' in order to do this. The method for this calculation is as follows:

```
# calculate daily returns
df['returns'] = np.log(df['Close'] /
df['Close'].shift(1))
df['returns'].fillna(0)
df['returns_1'] = df['returns'].fillna(0)
df['returns_2'] =
df['returns_1'].replace([np.inf, -np.inf],
np.nan)
df['returns_final'] = df['returns_2'].fillna(0)
```

Upon calculation of daily returns, we are now ready to apply our classification function for 1's and -1's to these returns. If the stock return for AMZN was positive, we assign a 1, and if it was negative, a -1. This is done with the following line of code:

```
df.iloc[:, len(df.columns) - 1] = df.iloc[:,
len(df.columns) -
1].apply(computeClassification)
```

Now that we have assigned our classification function to our dataset's closing returns, we can go ahead and begin the organizational process for our logistical regression machine learning model. This entails us deciding what percent of our dataset we want to train the machine learning model on, and what percent we want to test the model on. This is a very subjective aspect of machine learning, with no clear right or wrong answer. While many data scientists like to assign such proportions equally, others will tend to skew more heavily. For our specific example, we will train the machine learning model on 90% of our data, while forward testing its results on the remaining 10% of our data. Thus, employing a 90-10 train to test ratio. The process is done with the following lines

of code:

```python
# Compute the last column (Y) -1 = down, 1 = up
by applying the defined classifier above to the
'returns_final' dataframe
df.iloc[:, len(df.columns) - 1] = df.iloc[:,
len(df.columns) -
1].apply(computeClassification)


# Now that we have a complete dataset with a
predictable value, the last column "Return"
which is either -1 or 1, create the train and
test dataset.
# convert float to int so you can slice the
dataframe
testData = df[-int((len(df) * 0.10)):]   # 2nd
half is forward tested on
trainData = df[:-int((len(df) * 0.90))]   # 1st
half is trained on


# replace all inf with nan
testData_1 = testData.replace([np.inf, -np.inf],
np.nan)
trainData_1 = trainData.replace([np.inf, -
np.inf], np.nan)
# replace all nans with 0
testData_2 = testData_1.fillna(0)
trainData_2 = trainData_1.fillna(0)
```

```
# X is the list of features
data_X_train = trainData_2.iloc[:,
0:len(trainData_2.columns) - 1]
# Y is the 1 or -1 value to be predicted (as we
added this for the last column above using the
apply.(computeClassification) function
data_Y_train = trainData_2.iloc[:,
len(trainData_2.columns) - 1]

# Same thing for the test dataset
data_X_test = testData_2.iloc[:,
0:len(testData_2.columns) - 1]
data_Y_test = testData_2.iloc[:,
len(testData_2.columns) - 1]
```

We are now finally ready to employ our logistical regression ML model to our dataset for AMZN. As mentioned before, we will be using python's scikit-learn library in order to do this. The first step will be to import necessary libraries from scikit-learn:

```
from sklearn.linear_model import
LogisticRegression
# DEFINE METHOD FOR PRINTING TRAIN AND TEST
ACCURACY SCORE
from sklearn.model_selection import
cross_val_score, cross_val_predict
from sklearn.metrics import accuracy_score,
classification_report, confusion_matrix
```

The above imports allow us to set up our model parameters, along with testing configurations that enable us to analyze how well our model did in terms of price prediction for AMZN. Additionally, we can create a function, we will call print_score, that will allow us to assess the accuracy score for our model in terms of price prediction. This function is as follows:

```
def print_score(clf, data_X_train, data_y_train,
data_X_test, data_y_test, train=True):
    '''
    print the accuracy score, classification
report and confusion matrix of classifier
    '''
    if train:
        '''
        training performance
        '''
        print("Train Result:\n")
        print("accuracy score:
{0:.4f}\n".format(accuracy_score(data_y_train,
clf.predict(data_X_train))))
        print("Classification Report: \n
{}\n".format(classification_report(data_y_train,
clf.predict(data_X_train))))
        print("Confusion Matrix: \n
{}\n".format(confusion_matrix(data_y_train,
```

```
clf.predict(data_X_train))))


        res = cross_val_score(clf, data_X_train,
data_y_train, cv=10, scoring='accuracy')
        print("Average Accuracy: \t
{0:.4f}".format(np.mean(res)))
        print("Accuracy SD: \t\t
{0:.4f}".format(np.std(res)))


    elif train == False:
        '''
        test performance
        '''
        print("Test Result:\n")
        print("accuracy score:
{0:.4f}\n".format(accuracy_score(data_y_test,
clf.predict(data_X_test))))
        print("Classification Report: \n
{}\n".format(classification_report(data_y_test,
clf.predict(data_X_test))))
        print("Confusion Matrix: \n
{}\n".format(confusion_matrix(data_y_test,
clf.predict(data_X_test))))
```

We are now ready to apply the built in logistical regression classifier within python's scikit-learn library to our dataset for AMZN. In order to do so, we must first assign the classifier to a variable name, fit our training data for x (which is our predictor variables of open, high, low, and close) and our training data for y (simply, the close prices that we are trying to predict by using our classification method). This is done with the following lines of code:

```
# logistic regression
clf = LogisticRegression()


clf.fit(data_X_train, data_Y_train)


# predictions is an array containing the
predicted values (-1 or 1) for the features in
data_X_test.
# You can see the prediction accuracy using the
method accuracy_score which compares the
predicted values versus the expected ones.

from sklearn.metrics import accuracy_score

y_predictions = clf.predict(data_X_test)   #
predict y based on x_test
print("Accuracy Score Employing Machine
Learning: " + str(accuracy_score(data_Y_test,
y_predictions)))
```

And in terms of classifying how well our model can predict the close price for AMZN, that is pretty much it. Running the code up through this segment will display results similar to the following:

Accuracy Score Employing Machine Learning: 0.5315315315315315

Telling us that essentially, for AMZN and our given time period employing a 90-10 train to test ratio, the logistic regression machine learning model was able to predict the close price for AMZN at an approx. 53% accuracy rate. While it may not be as much above the 50% threshold as desires, we can definitely see that there is something there in terms of a simple model such as this being able to employ logistical regression and mathematics to price prediction. Next, we will take our algorithm a step forward and create a simple backtest function that attempts to monitor and judge how well we would have done if we actually traded on our model for the specific test period in question, being roughly 10% of our data. Which amounts to roughly 222 trading days for AMZN, with the last day being October 29, 2018. In other words, going back from October 29, 2018 222 trading days in time.

APPLYING PYTHON'S FFN MODULE TO BACKTEST TRADING SIGNALS FOR AMZN

Now that we have our logistical regression model in place, the next step will be to apply a commonly used library in python called ffn to our dataset, in attempt to backtest how we could have done if we traded on our machine learning signals. Before we do so, we will add one final step in which we calculate a 200 day moving average for AMZN, to add as an extra layer of conviction, or filter, for our signals. In short, now not only does our machine learning signal have to return a 1 for us to buy, but the closing price for AMZN must always be above its 200 day moving average as well. And vice versa, in order to signal a sell, both the machine learning model must return -1, and the closing price for AMZN must be below the 200 day moving average. The code required to set this up is as follows:

```
df['SMA'] = df['Close'].rolling(200).mean()   # calculate n period SMA

df['Sell1'] = df['Close'] < df['SMA']
df['SELL'] = df['Sell1']
```

```
df['Buy1'] = df['Close'] > df['SMA']
df['BUY'] = df['Buy1']


buy_technical_signal = df['BUY'][-222:]   #
extract last n daily signals
sell_technical_signal = df['SELL'][-222:]   #
extract last n daily signals
print("buy technical signal length",
len(buy_technical_signal))
print("sell technical signal length",
len(sell_technical_signal))
print("buy technical signal",
buy_technical_signal)
print("sell technical signal",
sell_technical_signal)
buy_technical_signal =
pd.DataFrame(buy_technical_signal)
sell_technical_signal =
pd.DataFrame(sell_technical_signal)



pred = pd.DataFrame(predictions_dataframe)
print("prediction", pred)
print("PREDICTION LENGTH",
len(predictions_dataframe))

pred['Signal'] = 0
```

```python
# reindex data for later concatenation into 1
DataFrame - will all need same index to concat
properly
buy_technical_signal.set_index(pred.index,
inplace=True)
sell_technical_signal.set_index(pred.index,
inplace=True)

# set up filters
filter1 = (predictions_dataframe[0] > 0)   #
first buy filter (deep learning one)
filter2 = buy_technical_signal > 0  # second buy
filter (technical one), > 0 implies argument is
true (1)
filter3 = (predictions_dataframe[0]) < 0   #
first sell filter (deep learning one)
filter4 = sell_technical_signal > 0  # second
sell filter (technical one), > 0 implies
argument is true (1)

# concatenate all data into 1 DataFrame for easy
viewing/confirmation
pred2 = pd.concat([pred, buy_technical_signal,
sell_technical_signal, filter1, filter2,
filter3, filter4], axis=1)
pred2.columns = ['Pred', 'Signal', 'Buy Tech
Signal', 'Sell Tech Signal', 'Filter1',
'Filter2', 'Filter3', 'Filter4']

# use np.where function to set Signal according
```

```python
to whether above filters are satisfied
pred2['Signal'] = np.where(pred2['Filter1'] &
pred2['Filter2'], 1, 0)
pred2['Signal'] = np.where(pred2['Filter3'] &
pred2['Filter4'], -1, pred2['Signal'])


buys = pred2.loc[pred2['Signal'] == 1]
sells = pred2.loc[pred2['Signal'] == -1]


# need to reindex the buys and sells DataFrames
to match the index of 'df[Close]'
if not buys.empty:
    buy_index_new = buys.index[-1] - buys.index
    buy_index_new_2 = len(df.index) -
buy_index_new
    buys.set_index(buy_index_new_2,
inplace=True)


if not sells.empty:
    sell_index_new = sells.index[-1] -
sells.index
    sell_index_new_2 = len(df.index) -
sell_index_new
    sells.set_index(sell_index_new_2,
inplace=True)




# iloc[row slicing, column slicing] Real Stock
```

```python
Price set to last n days of stock's close price
real_stock_price = df.iloc[-222:,3]   # first -n:
element is length of predictions, 3rd column is
close prices
real_stock_price = real_stock_price.values
real_stock_price =
pd.DataFrame(real_stock_price)   # convert to
pandas data frame
print(real_stock_price)
print("REAL STOCK PRICE", real_stock_price)


# Visualize strategy with a chart


# the buys and sells have integer range indices
(i.e. 1,2,3....) whereas the df index has
datetime values. Reindex df using:
df.set_index(pd.RangeIndex(0, len(df)),
inplace=True)


# plot price
plt.plot(df.index, df['Close'], label='Asset')


# Plot the buy and sell signals on the same plot


plt.plot(sells.index,
df.loc[sells.index]['Close'], 'v',
markersize=10, color='r')
plt.plot(buys.index,
df.loc[buys.index]['Close'], '^', markersize=10,
```

```
color='g')
plt.ylabel('Price')
plt.xlabel('Date')
plt.legend(loc=0)
# Display everything
plt.show()
```

Our final step will be to create a backtest function and employ python's ffn module to it, so that we can gain a deeper understanding on how well we could have predicted AMZN price returns using our logistical regression machine learning framework. Further information on this module can be found at:

https://pypi.org/project/ffn/

Before we can employ the ffn module to backtest results, we must create a basic backtesting function to use on the data. We will set the starting cash on the portfolio to $100,000. The function looks like the following:

```
# BACKTESTING
# define backtest method
def backtest(data):
    cash = 100000  # set starting cash to
$100,000
    position = 0  # set position to 0 for
```

current number of shares

```
    total = 0
    equity_curve_df = []
    data['Total'] = 100000  # start with 100k
for our strategy
    # To compute the Buy and Hold value, I
invest all of my cash in X asset on the first
day of the backtest
    increment = 10  # number of shares


    for row in data.iterrows():
        price = float(row[1][0])  # Remember
that "iterrows" returns an indexer(i.e.
0,1,2,3,4....)  and the row of the DataFrame in
a row vector - so you need to also reference the
column you want in the row vector, hence the
[1][3] - the 1 being the row (rather than the
indexer), and the column within that row.
        signal = pred2.iloc[row[0]][1]  # signal
for our strategy, 2nd column in the dataframe is
signals of 1 and -1



        if (signal > 0 and cash - increment *
price > 0):  # ensure signal is 1 (or > 0), and
there is enough cash to place trade (100,000 -
(1,000 * price of asset) > 0 )
            # Buy
            cash = cash - increment * price   #
deduct how many shares we bought and update cash
```

remaining value

```
                position = position + increment   #
position is 0 + 1,000 shares (this keeps on
going and looping as long as cash is available
for another buy, assuming signal is there)
                # print(row[0].strftime('%d %b %Y')
+ " Position = " + str(position) + " Cash = " +
str(cash) + " // Total =
{:,}".format(int(position * price + cash)))



        elif (signal < 0 and abs(position *
price) < cash):   # ensure signal is -1 (or < 0),
and absolute value of (position or shares sold *
price of stock is less than cash value to allow
trade)
                # Sell
                cash = cash + increment * price   #
add cash value of portfolio to how many shares
we sold, and update cash remaining value
                position = position - increment   #
position is new position (number of shares) -
increment (or how many shares were sold)
                # print(row[0].strftime('%d %b %Y')
+ " Position = " + str(position) + " Cash = " +
str(cash) + " // Total =
{:,}".format(int(position * price + cash)))


        # data.loc[data.index == row[0],
'Total'] = float(position * price + cash)   #
```

```
return number of shares multiplied by price of
asset + cash left in balance

        equity_curve_df.append(float(position *
price + cash))

    # equity_curve_df =
pd.DataFrame(equity_curve_df,index=range(len(equ
ity_curve_df)),columns=["Total"])
    index = pd.date_range('11/01/2017',
periods=len(equity_curve_df), freq='D')
    equity_curve_df =
pd.DataFrame(equity_curve_df, index=index,
columns=['Total'])
    return equity_curve_df  # return number of
shares multiplied by price of asset + cash left
in balance
```

Finally, we can apply the ffn module to our defined backtest function to display the results of the strategy as follows:

```
# Backtest for our strategy to create equity
curve df by running backtest function defined
above
equity_curve_df = backtest(real_stock_price)  #
for our strategy, backtest will be equal to the
backtest(data) method we define above, utilizing
our dataframe as the data
```

```
print(equity_curve_df)  # prints out cash value
of backtest result in USD

#
*****************************************************
*****************************************************
*****************************************************
*****************************************************
******************************

# Apply Financial Functions for Python (FFN) to
calculate statistics of algorithm
equity_curve_df['Equity'] = equity_curve_df
perf = equity_curve_df['Equity'].calc_stats()

# plot equity curve
perf.plot()
plt.show()

# show overall metrics
perf.display()

# display monthly returns
perf.display_monthly_returns()

# plotting visual representation of strategy
drawdown series:
ffn.to_drawdown_series(equity_curve_df['Equity']
).plot(figsize=(15, 7), grid=True)
#plt.show()
```

```
# plot histogram of returns
perf.plot_histogram()
#plt.show()

# extract lookback returns
#perf.display_lookback_returns()

print("Accuracy Score: " +
str(accuracy_score(data_Y_test, y_predictions)))
# print_score(clf, data_X_train, data_Y_train,
data_X_test, data_Y_test, train=True) # set to
True for training
print_score(clf, data_X_train, data_Y_train,
data_X_test, data_Y_test,train=False)  # set to
False because we want testing now



print("CURRENT SIGNAL FOR SECURITY (1 FOR BUY, -
1 FOR SELL, 0 FOR NEUTRAL):")
print(pred2.iloc[:,0])
```

The output for our code will create an equity price curve for how our initial $100,00 starting portfolio value would have faired through our specified testing period. Which for us, was 222 trading days going back from October 29, 2018. The equity price curve created by python looks like the following:

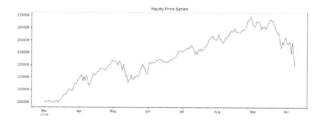

The associated actual backtest results created through the ffn module will look like:

Summary:								
Total Return		Sharpe	CAGR		Max Drawdown			
28.98%		1.15	52.29%		-23.69%			

Annualized Returns:								
mtd	3m	6m	ytd	1y	3y	5y	10y	incep.
-15.37%	-10.83%	8.19%	28.98%	-	-	-	-	52.29%

The final line of code in our algorithm, being:

```
print("CURRENT SIGNAL FOR SECURITY (1 FOR BUY, -
1 FOR SELL, 0 FOR NEUTRAL):")
print(pred2.iloc[:,0])
```

allows us to simply notice what the latest, or current signal based on the last data point of our dataset is for AMZN; 1 buying buy, and -1 being sell.

And in terms of logistical regression machine learning applied to a specific stock, that is pretty much it. Very simple for the most part to code up. The ffn module allowed us to take this algorithm and apply historical statistics to it, so that we can gain a better understanding of how we could have done by acting on its signals. For the next section, we will go ahead and apply a much different technique employing artificial intelligence as a means of comparison to this model for AMZN, and see if we can beat our current results. This will be done through a probabilistic approach, employing deep learning with python's keras module.

KERAS CNN MODEL FOR DEEP LEARNING PREDICTIONS ON AMZN

Now, let us go ahead and compare the results from our logistical regression machine learning model for AMZN to a deep learning neural network approach, employing python's popular keras CNN convolution neural network. Further information on this model can be found at:

https://keras.io/layers/convolutional/

In general, deep learning refers to neural networks with multiple hidden layers that can learning increasingly abstract representations of the input data. For this specific example, we will again take AMZN for the same time span of January 1, 2010 through October 29, 2018, and apply a CNN framework that attempts to predict closing prices through a probabilistic model. These thresholds of probability (i.e. conviction levels) will be coded in a subjective manner, upon which the user can alter to meet his or her specific parameter needs. For CNN models such as this, you generally have a series of inputs (convolutions), feature maps (sub-sampling) and fully connected output layers. While CNNs have typically been

34

used more for image recognition utilizing artificial intelligence in the past, they have slowly made their way into the financial spectrum recently; and definitely showing promising signs. For this specific example employing a CNN approach, we will use an 80-20 train test split ratio, in which we train on approx. 80% of our data, while testing on approx. 20%. This 20% amounts to approx. 439 trading days going back from October 29, 2018 (the last day in our data set).

In order to properly organize our training and testing data for the CNN algorithm, we will create a short script called 'utils.py', that will allow us to preprocess our dataset so that python can correctly interpret how to design and utilize the CNN model. Most importantly, this utils.py file is essential and required as a dependence for our algorithm to run off. The script written for this utils.py file is as follows:

```python
def shuffle_in_unison(a, b):
    # courtesy
http://stackoverflow.com/users/190280/josh-
bleecher-snyder
    assert len(a) == len(b)
    shuffled_a = np.empty(a.shape,
dtype=a.dtype)
```

```
    shuffled_b = np.empty(b.shape,
dtype=b.dtype)
    permutation = np.random.permutation(len(a))
    for old_index, new_index in
enumerate(permutation):
        shuffled_a[new_index] = a[old_index]
        shuffled_b[new_index] = b[old_index]
    return shuffled_a, shuffled_b


def create_Xt_Yt(X, y, percentage=0.80): # test
on n% of the data. When was at 0.8, was testing
on 20% of the data, 0.477 to get pred = 362 for
q learning q trader algo
    p = int(len(X) * percentage)
    X_train = X[0:p]
    Y_train = y[0:p]

    X_train, Y_train =
shuffle_in_unison(X_train, Y_train)

    X_test = X[p:]
    Y_test = y[p:]

    return X_train, X_test, Y_train, Y_test


def remove_nan_examples(data):
    newX = []
    for i in range(len(data)):
```

```
    if np.isnan(data[i]).any() == False:
        newX.append(data[i])
return newX
```

Similar to our first model employing logistical regression machine learning, our CNN deep learning model employing keras needs to first read in all of the required libraries:

```
from utils import *

import pandas as pd
import matplotlib.pylab as plt

from keras.models import Sequential
from keras.layers.core import Dense, Dropout,
Activation, Flatten
from keras.layers.recurrent import LSTM, GRU
from keras.layers import Convolution1D,
MaxPooling1D, AtrousConvolution1D, RepeatVector
from keras.callbacks import ModelCheckpoint,
ReduceLROnPlateau, CSVLogger
from keras.layers.wrappers import Bidirectional
from keras import regularizers
from keras.layers.normalization import
BatchNormalization
from keras.layers.advanced_activations import *
from keras.optimizers import RMSprop, Adam, SGD,
Nadam
```

37

```
from keras.initializers import *
import ffn
import seaborn as sns
sns.despine()
from math import sqrt
from pandas_datareader import data as pdr
import fix_yahoo_finance as yf
import datetime
yf.pdr_override()
```

Upon importing the installed libraries, we can go ahead and assign the required variable parameters to lists, which will be the open, high, low, close, and volume for AMZN.

```
openp = data_original.ix[:, 'Open'].tolist()
highp = data_original.ix[:, 'High'].tolist()
lowp = data_original.ix[:, 'Low'].tolist()
closep = data_original.ix[:, 'Adj
Close'].tolist()
volumep = data_original.ix[:, 'Volume'].tolist()

# data_chng = data_original.ix[:, 'Adj
Close'].pct_change().dropna().tolist()

WINDOW = 30 # 30 day windows
EMB_SIZE = 5 # number of features (open, high,
low, close, volume)
STEP = 1
FORECAST = 1 # forecasting 1 day out
```

```
X, Y = [], []
for i in range(0, len(data_original), STEP):
    try:
        o = openp[i:i+WINDOW]
        h = highp[i:i+WINDOW]
        l = lowp[i:i+WINDOW]
        c = closep[i:i+WINDOW]
        v = volumep[i:i+WINDOW]


        # remember, we are not necessarily
interested in predicting the exact value (thus,
the expected value and variance of the future
isn't very interesting (we just need to predict
the up or down movement).
        # normalize open, high, low, close, and
volume by subtracting mean, and dividing by
standard deviation
        o = (np.array(o) - np.mean(o)) /
np.std(o)
        h = (np.array(h) - np.mean(h)) /
np.std(h)
        l = (np.array(l) - np.mean(l)) /
np.std(l)
        c = (np.array(c) - np.mean(c)) /
np.std(c)
        v = (np.array(v) - np.mean(v)) /
np.std(v)


        # Since we want to forecast the
```

probability of moment either up or down the following day, we need to consider the change of a single dimension:

```
    x_i = closep[i:i+WINDOW] # closing price
of x values for the window of 30 days
    y_i = closep[i+WINDOW+FORECAST] #
closing price of y value (close) for the window
of 30 days, + a forecast of 1 day out

    last_close = x_i[-1] # previous day's
close
    next_close = y_i # predicted future
close 1 day out

    if last_close < next_close: # if next
(or future close price 1 day out) was greater
than prior day's close price.....
        y_i = [1, 0] # price went up with
100% probability
    else:
        y_i = [0, 1] # price went down with
100% probability


    x_i = np.column_stack((o, h, l, c, v)) #
stack columns for open, high, low, close, and
volume

    except Exception as e:
```

```
    break

  X.append(x_i)
  Y.append(y_i)
```

Next, we can go ahead and employ our created functions from our utils.py file in order to preprocess our data for the CNN algorithm, so that python will be able to correctly assess how to structure and prepare the framework to run properly. Done as follows:

```
X, Y = np.array(X), np.array(Y)
X_train, X_test, Y_train, Y_test =
create_Xt_Yt(X, Y) # utilize function from
utils.py to create x train, x test, y train, y
test , see method 'def create_Xt_Yt' in
utils.py: we are training on 90% , and testing
on 10%

# scale data
X_train = np.reshape(X_train, (X_train.shape[0],
X_train.shape[1], EMB_SIZE))
X_test = np.reshape(X_test, (X_test.shape[0],
X_test.shape[1], EMB_SIZE))
```

Similar to our prior model, for additional trading conviction, we will code up some technical indicators that

41

can be added to the neural network as a means of providing us with additional trading signals of higher probability. We will allow for the possibility of including simple moving averages, standard deviations, Bollinger bands, MACD, RSI, and momentum. The can be coded as follows:

```
# TECHNICAL INDICATORS

data_original['Stdev'] = data_original['Adj
Close'].rolling(window=90).std()   # calculate
rolling std
data_original['SMA'] = data_original['Adj
Close'].rolling(100).mean()   # calculate n tick
SMA


# Bollinger Bands
data_original['Upper Band'] =
data_original['SMA'] + (data_original['Stdev'] *
1)   # 1 standard deviations above
data_original['Lower Band'] =
data_original['SMA'] - (data_original['Stdev'] *
1)   # 1 standard deviations below


# MACD 12,26,9
data_original['stock_df_12_ema'] =
pd.ewma(data_original['Close'], span=12)
data_original['stock_df_26_ema'] =
pd.ewma(data_original['Close'], span=26)
```

```python
data_original['stock_df_macd_12_26'] =
data_original['stock_df_12_ema'] -
data_original['stock_df_26_ema']
data_original['stock_df_signal_12_26'] =
pd.ewma(data_original['stock_df_macd_12_26'],
span=9)
data_original['stock_df_crossover_12_26'] =
data_original['stock_df_macd_12_26'] -
data_original['stock_df_signal_12_26'] # means,
# if this is > 0, or stock_df['Crossover'] =
# stock_df['MACD'] - stock_df['Signal'] > 0, there
# is a buy signal

# means, if this is < 0, or
# stock_df['Crossover'] =  stock_df['MACD'] -
# stock_df['Signal'] < 0, there is a sell signal


# RSI
def RSI(series, period):
    delta = series.diff().dropna()
    u = delta * 0
    d = u.copy()
    u[delta > 0] = delta[delta > 0]
    d[delta < 0] = -delta[delta < 0]
    u[u.index[period - 1]] = np.mean(u[:period])
# first value is sum of avg gains
    u = u.drop(u.index[:(period - 1)])
    d[d.index[period - 1]] = np.mean(d[:period])
# first value is sum of avg losses
    d = d.drop(d.index[:(period - 1)])
```

```
    rs = pd.stats.moments.ewma(u, com=period -
1, adjust=False) / \
            pd.stats.moments.ewma(d, com=period
- 1, adjust=False)
    return 100 - 100 / (1 + rs)



data_original['RSI'] = RSI(data_original['Adj
Close'],14)  # RSI function of series defined by
the close price, and period of choosing
(defaulted to 14)

# calculate daily returns
data_original['returns'] =
np.log(data_original['Adj Close'] /
data_original['Adj Close'].shift(1))
data_original['returns'].fillna(0)
data_original['returns_1'] =
data_original['returns'].fillna(0)
data_original['returns_2'] =
data_original['returns_1'].replace([np.inf, -
np.inf], np.nan)
data_original['returns_final'] =
data_original['returns_2'].fillna(0)
# Momentum setup for parameters over a rolling
mean time window of 2 ( i.e average of past two
day returns)
data_original['mom'] =
np.sign(data_original['returns_final'].rolling(5
).mean())
```

Now that we have properly pre processed our data for AMZN, we are ready to create and apply our CNN deep learning neural network to the data. We have chosen the CNN model specifically for its flexibility and interpretability of hyper parameters. We will apply the CNN framework to a sequential model, train our data, and finally compute our model accuracy and loss estimates using keras. This is done in the following manner:

Models in Keras can come in two forms – Sequential and via the Functional API. For most deep learning networks that you build, the Sequential model is likely what you will use.

This allows you to easily stack sequential layers (and even recurrent layers) of the network in order from input to output. The functional API allows you to build more complicated architectures.

model = Sequential() *Configures the model for training*

1st layer of the 1D Convolution, i.e. temporal convolution. This layer creates a convolution kernel that is convolved with the layer input over a single spatial dimension to produce a tensor of outputs.

Also, notice that we don't have to declare any weights or bias variables like we do in TensorFlow, as Keras sorts that out for us.

```
model.add(Convolution1D(input_shape = (WINDOW,
EMB_SIZE),
```
 # 3D tensor with shape: (samples, steps, input_dim). For us, windows = 30 is steps and EMB_SIZE = 5 is input_dim.

```
                        nb_filter=16,
```
nb_filter: Number of convolution kernels to use (dimensionality of the output)

```
                        filter_length=4,
```
The extension (spatial or temporal) of each filter.

```
                        border_mode='same'))
```
 # : 'valid', 'same', or 'full' ('full' requires the Theano backend).

.

```
model.add(BatchNormalization())
```
Normalize the activations of the previous layer at each batch, i.e. applies a transformation that maintains the mean activation close to 0 and the activation standard deviation close to 1.

```
model.add(LeakyReLU())
```
The rectifier is an activation function (what defines the output of

a node given an input or set of inputs). Leaky version of a Rectified Linear Unit. Leaky ReLUs allow a small, non-zero gradient when the unit is not active.

Leaky ReLUs are one attempt to fix the "dying ReLU" problem. Instead of the function being zero when x < 0, a leaky ReLU will instead have a small negative slope (of 0.01, or so)

That is, the function:
computes $f(x)=\mathbb{1}(x<0)(\alpha x)+\mathbb{1}(x>=0)(x)$ where α is a small constant. Some people report success with this form of activation function, but the results are not always consistent.

model.add(Dropout(0.5)) *# fraction of neurons (inputs) to drop. goal for dropout is to help neural network not overfit the data. We randomly deactivate 50% of certain units (neurons) in each layer by setting some of the dimensions in our input vector to be zero with probability keep_prob.*

Thus the neural network will continue to learn different. Training thus will be faster.

2nd Layer, no input shape given (only needed to be defined in 1st layer above)

47

```
model.add(Convolution1D(nb_filter=8,
                        filter_length=4,
                        border_mode='same'))
model.add(BatchNormalization())
model.add(LeakyReLU())
model.add(Dropout(0.5))
```

model.add(Flatten()) *This operation flattens the input (or rows of a 3D matrix). It does not affect the batch size. Flatten() operator unrolls the values beginning at the last dimension.*

INPUT LAYER
model.add(Dense(64)) *Dense(64) is a fully-connected layer with 64 hidden units. A dense layer represents a matrix vector multiplication. (assuming your batch size is 1)*

The values in the matrix are the trainable parameters which get updated during backpropagation. A dense layer thus is used to change the dimensions of your vector.

Mathematically speaking, it applies a rotation, scaling, translation
transform to your vector. In simple terms, A

dense layer is just a regular layer of neurons in a neural network. Each neuron recieves input from all the neurons in the previous layer, thus densely connected. The layer has a weight matrix W, a bias vector b, and the activations of previous layer a.

```
model.add(BatchNormalization())
model.add(LeakyReLU())
```

OUTPUT LAYER
```
model.add(Dense(2)) # Dense(64) is a fully-
```
connected layer with 2 hidden units.
```
model.add(Activation('softmax')) We apply the
```
softmax activation function; typically used for models with probabilistic approach, such as this.

2.COMPILE THE NEURAL NETWORK MODEL

```
opt = Nadam(lr=0.002)   # Define optimizer. We
```
will use the Nadam optimizer.
https://keras.io/optimizers/. Much like Adam is essentially RMSprop with momentum, Nadam is Adam RMSprop with Nesterov momentum.

Adapting the learning rate for your stochastic gradient descent optimization procedure can increase performance and reduce training time. Thus, the simplest and perhaps most used adaptation of learning rate during training are techniques that reduce the learning rate over time. These have the benefit of making large changes at the beginning of the training procedure when larger learning rate values are used, and decreasing the learning rate such that a smaller rate and therefore smaller training updates are made to weights later in the training procedure.

This training procedure has the effect of quickly learning good weights early and fine tuning them later. Two popular and easy to use learning rate schedules are as follows:

A. Decrease the learning rate gradually based on the epoch.
B. Decrease the learning rate using punctuated large drops at specific epochs.

The following are a few arguments for optimizers:
1. lr: learning rate, float >= 0.
2. beta_1, beta_2: floats, 0 < beta < 1. Generally close to 1.

*3. epsilon: float > = 0. Fuzz factor. If None,
defaults to K.epsilon().*

```
reduce_lr = ReduceLROnPlateau(monitor='val_acc',
factor=0.9, patience=30, min_lr=0.000001,
verbose=1)
```
https://keras.io/callbacks/#reducelronplateau.

*Reduce learning rate by a pre-defined factor
when a metric has stopped improving:
Models often benefit from reducing the learning
rate by a factor of 2-10 once learning
stagnates. This callback monitors a quantity and
if no improvement is seen for a 'patience'
number of epochs, the learning rate is reduced.*

*Arguments include:
1. monitor: quantity to be monitored
2. factor: factor by which the learning rate
will be reduced. new_lr = lr * factor
3. patience: number of epochs with no
improvement after which learning rate will be
reduced.
4. verbose: int. 0: quiet, 1: update messages.
5. min_lr: lower bound on the learning rate.*

```
checkpointer =
ModelCheckpoint(filepath="lolkek.hdf5",
verbose=1, save_best_only=True)
```
Checkpoint allows us to save the model after every epoch. It creates a custom callback by extending the base class keras.callbacks.Callback. A callback has access to its associated model through the class property self.model.

Arguments for this method include:
1. filepath: string, path to save the model file.
2. monitor: quantity to monitor.
3. verbose: verbosity mode, 0 or 1.
4. save_best_only: if save_best_only=True, the latest best model according to the quantity monitored will not be overwritten.

```
model.compile(optimizer=opt,
```
Optimization is whatever we set optimizer to
```
              loss='categorical_crossentropy',
```
https://keras.io/losses/ . Decide which loss function will be applied. The actual optimized objective is the mean of the output array across all data points.
```
              metrics=['accuracy'])
```
https://keras.io/metrics/ . Goal is to return a single tensor value representing the mean of the

output array across all data points.

```
history = model.fit(X_train, Y_train, Fit the
model using X_train, and Y_train data.
https://keras.io/models/sequential/
         nb_epoch = 100,  Number of epochs to
train the model. An epoch is an iteration over
the entire x and y data provided.
         batch_size = 128, Number of samples
per gradient update. If unspecified, it will
default to 32.
         verbose=1, Show updated messages when
set to 1.  0 = silent, 1 = progress bar.
         validation_data=(X_test, Y_test),
Tuple (x_val, y_val) or tuple (x_val, y_val,
val_sample_weights) on which to evaluate the
loss and any model metrics at the end of each
epoch. The model will not be trained on this
data. This will override validation_split.
         callbacks=[reduce_lr, checkpointer],
List of keras.callbacks.Callback instances. List
of callbacks to apply during training.
         shuffle=True) Shuffle: Boolean
(whether to shuffle the training data before
each epoch) or str (for 'batch'). 'batch' is a
special option for dealing with the limitations
of HDF5 data; it shuffles in batch-sized chunks.
Has no effect when steps_per_epoch is not  None.
```

3. PREDICT MODEL OUTPUT FOR OUT OF SAMPLE Y_TEST

model.load_weights("lolkek.hdf5") *Loads the weights of the model from a HDF5 file (created by save_weights). By default, the architecture is expected to be unchanged.*
https://keras.io/models/about-keras-models/
pred = model.predict(np.array(X_test)) *Predict output for out of sample Y_test, setting X_test (our out of sample features) to a numpy array*

USE CONFUSION MATRIX TO HELP CHECK FOR OVERFITTING:

```
from sklearn.metrics import
classification_report
from sklearn.metrics import confusion_matrix
C = confusion_matrix([np.argmax(y) for y in
Y_test], [np.argmax(y) for y in pred])

print(C / C.astype(np.float).sum(axis=1))
```

Example of a Classification output would be as follows:
[[0.75510204 0.24489796]

[0.46938776   0.53061224]]

*In which we forecasted up movements with 75%,
and down movements with 53% , off diagonal
elements are those mislabeled by the classifier.*

*And finally, we can plot our model loss and
accuracy for our training and testing data as
follows:*

PLOT MODEL LOSS & ACCURACY

```
plt.figure()
plt.plot(history.history['loss'])
plt.plot(history.history['val_loss'])
plt.title('model loss')
plt.ylabel('loss')
plt.xlabel('epoch')
plt.legend(['train', 'test'], loc='best')
plt.show()

plt.figure()
plt.plot(history.history['acc'])
plt.plot(history.history['val_acc'])
plt.title('model accuracy')
plt.ylabel('accuracy')
plt.xlabel('epoch')
plt.legend(['train', 'test'], loc='best')
plt.show()
```

The code runs through multiple iterations as defined by our epochs and batch sizes above, and subsequently generates a nice plot for both model loss and accuracy on our testing period of approx. 439 trading days as follows:

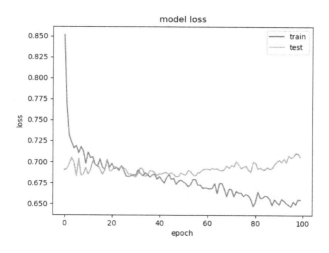

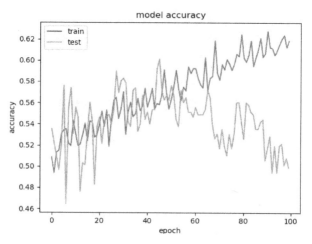

Now that we have applied the CNN model to our dataset successfully, we are able to go ahead and code specific technical indicators (that recall we defined before) into the CNN framework. This can be done in the following manner:

```
df_close = data_original['Adj Close'][-
439:].reset_index(drop=True)
df_SMA = data_original['SMA'][-
439:].reset_index(drop=True)
df_mom = data_original['mom'][-
439:].reset_index(drop=True)
df_MACD =
data_original['stock_df_crossover_12_26'][-
439:].reset_index(drop=True)
df_RSI = data_original['RSI'][-
439:].reset_index(drop=True)
df_upper_band = data_original['Upper Band'][-
439:].reset_index(drop=True)
df_lower_band = data_original['Lower Band'][-
439:].reset_index(drop=True)


df_buy1 = df_close > df_SMA

df_buy2 = df_mom > 0

df_buy3 = df_RSI < 55
```

```
df_buy4 = df_MACD > 0


df_BUY = df_buy1 + df_buy2 + df_buy3 + df_buy4
df_BUY_FINAL = df_BUY.reset_index(drop=True)



df_sell1 = df_close < df_SMA

df_sell2 = df_mom < 0

df_sell3 = df_RSI > 50

df_sell4 = df_MACD < 0


df_SELL = df_sell1 + df_sell2 + df_sell3 +
df_sell4
df_SELL_FINAL = df_SELL.reset_index(drop=True)
```

And now onto probably the most crucial part of this CNN framework, which is where we actually go ahead and assign a probability threshold to when we want our buy and sell signals to appear. For this particular example on AMZN, we have defined these key levels as 0.57 and 0.41. Meaning, if the algorithm generates a probability of 57%

or more that the signal is going to be a buy, we buy. And contrarily, if it generates a probability that the buy signal is only at 41% or more, we actually go ahead and sell. The generally underlying notion here being that we only want to buy AMZN if the probability of it going up tomorrow is above a certain threshold, being 57% in this case. Again, these levels can be altered to whatever one wants when playing around with the algorithm and fine tuning results. Additionally, recall we have also coded in technical indicators as an extra layer of conviction for our trading signals. As shown above in the prior block of code, for this example, these include simple moving averages, momentum, RSI, and MACD. All of which must unanimously point to a buy or a sell in addition to the CNNs signals in order for a trade to pass prerequisites and actually take place.

The code associated with this is as follows:

```
#set up filters
filter1 = (pred[0] > 0.57) # buy filter, 1st
column [0] of pred dataframe (recall 2nd column
[1] is simply % that stock will drop)
filter2 = (pred[0] < 0.41) # sell filter, 1st
column [0] of pred dataframe (recall 2nd column
[1] is simply % that stock will drop#)
filter3 = buy_technical_signal > 0  # second buy
```

```
filter (technical one), > 0 implies argument is
true (1)
filter4 = sell_technical_signal > 0   # second
sell filter (technical one), > 0 implies
argument is true (1)

#concatenate all data into 1 DataFrame for easy
viewing/confirmationpip
pred2 = pd.concat([pred,filter1,filter2,
filter3, filter4],axis=1)
print(pred2)
pred2.columns = ['Pred 1st Column','Pred 2nd
Column','Signal','Filter1','Filter2', 'Filter3',
'Filter4']


#use np.where function to set Signal according
to whether above filters are satisfied
pred2['Signal'] = np.where(pred2['Filter1'] &
pred2['Filter3'],1,0)
pred2['Signal'] = np.where(pred2['Filter2'] &
pred2['Filter4'],-1,pred2['Signal'])



buys = pred2.loc[pred2['Signal'] == 1]
sells = pred2.loc[pred2['Signal'] == -1]


# need to reindex the buys and sells DataFrames
to match the index of 'data_original[Close]'
if not buys.empty:
    buy_index_new = buys.index[-1] - buys.index
    buy_index_new_2 = len(data_original.index) -
buy_index_new
    buys.set_index(buy_index_new_2,inplace=True)

if not sells.empty:
    sell_index_new = sells.index[-1] -
```

```
sells.index
    sell_index_new_2 = len(data_original.index)
- sell_index_new

sells.set_index(sell_index_new_2,inplace=True)



# iloc[row slicing, column slicing] Real Stock
Price set to last 788 days of stock's close
price
real_stock_price = data_original.iloc[-439:,4] #
length of predictions_dataframe is the last
1,607 days when training at 80%, testing 20% of
total data . 4th column is close prices
real_stock_price = real_stock_price.values
real_stock_price =
pd.DataFrame(real_stock_price) # convert to
pandas data frame
print(real_stock_price)
print("REAL STOCK PRICE",real_stock_price)
```

Our algorithm is now finally setup to begin backtesting. Similar to before, we will see the starting portfolio value at $100,000, and implement a similar backtest function as our logistic regression model, in attempt to see if we can beat our initial model's performance by employing our new CNN neural network to AMZN during the same time period. Again, we will first write the backtesting function, and then as before apply python's ffn module to it for results. Done as follows:

```
# define backtest method
def backtest(data):
    cash = 100000 # set starting cash to
$100,000
    position = 0 # set position to 0 for current
number of shares
    total = 0
    equity_curve_df = []


    data['Total'] = 100000 # start with 100k for
our strategy
    # To compute the Buy and Hold value, I
invest all of my cash in X asset on the first
day of the backtest
    increment = 50 # number of shares


    for row in data.iterrows():
        price = float(row[1][0]) # Remember that
"iterrows" returns an indexer(i.e.
0,1,2,3,4....)  and the row of the DataFrame in
a row vector - so you need to also reference the
column you want in the row vector, hence the
[1][3] - the 1 being the row (rather than the
indexer), and the column within that row.
        signal = pred2.iloc[row[0]][2]  # signal
for our strategy, 3rd column in the pred2
dataframe is signals of 1 and -1



        if (signal > 0 and cash - increment *
```

```
price > 0): # ensure signal is 1 (or > 0), and
there is enough cash to place trade (100,000 -
(1,000 * price of asset) > 0 )
            # Buy
            cash = cash - increment * price #
deduct how many shares we bought and update cash
remaining value
            position = position + increment #
position is 0 + 1,000 shares (this keeps on
going and looping as long as cash is available
for another buy, assuming signal is there)
            #print(row[0].strftime('%d %b %Y') +
" Position = " + str(position) + " Cash = " +
str(cash) + " // Total =
{:,}".format(int(position * price + cash)))


        elif (signal < 0 and abs(position *
price) < cash): # ensure signal is -1 (or < 0),
and absolute value of (position or shares sold *
price of stock is less than cash value to allow
trade)
            # Sell
            cash = cash + increment * price #
add cash value of portfolio to how many shares
we sold, and update cash remaining value
            position = position - increment #
position is new position (number of shares) -
increment (or how many shares were sold)
            #print(row[0].strftime('%d %b %Y') +
" Position = " + str(position) + " Cash = " +
```

```
str(cash) + " // Total =
{:,}".format(int(position * price + cash)))

        equity_curve_df.append(float(position *
price + cash))

    # equity_curve_df =
pd.DataFrame(equity_curve_df,index=range(len(equ
ity_curve_df)),columns=["Total"])
    index = pd.date_range('03/01/2018',
periods=len(equity_curve_df), freq='D')
    equity_curve_df =
pd.DataFrame(equity_curve_df, index=index,
columns=['Total'])
    return equity_curve_df  # return number of
shares multiplied by price of asset + cash left
in balance


# Now, implement backtest method defined above:

# Backtest for our strategy to create equity
curve df by running backtest function defined
above
equity_curve_df  = backtest(real_stock_price) #
for our strategy, backtest will be equal to the
backtest(data) method we define above, utilizing
our dataframe as the data
print(equity_curve_df) # prints out cash value
of backtest result in USD
```

```
# Apply Financial Functions for Python (FFN) to
calculate statistics of algorithm
equity_curve_df['Equity'] = equity_curve_df
perf = equity_curve_df['Equity'].calc_stats()


# plot equity curve
perf.plot()
plt.show()

# show overall metrics
perf.display()


# display monthly returns
perf.display_monthly_returns()


# plotting visual representation of strategy
drawdown series:
ffn.to_drawdown_series(equity_curve_df['Equity']
).plot(figsize=(15,7),grid=True)
#plt.show()


# plot histogram of returns
perf.plot_histogram()
#plt.show()
```

```
# extract lookback returns
perf.display_lookback_returns()
```

```
# PRINT COLUMN OF SIGNALS FOR THE STRATEGY
print("CURRENT SIGNAL FOR ALGORITHM: 1: BUY, 0:
HOLD, -1:SELL")
print(pred2.iloc[:,2])
```

The model results, including our equity curve and backtest function were as follows:

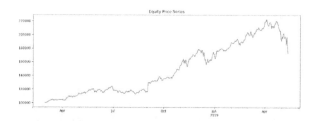

Comparing results from our CNN neural network to our initial logistical regression machine learning model, we immediately notice that the CNN model outperformed. Recall for the logistical regression model, total return was approx. 28.9%, compared to 73.0% for the CNN model. Ok, that is great, but what about drawdown? We notice that for the logistical regression model, drawdown was approx. -23.6% with a Sharpe of 1.15. When compared to our new CNN model, drawdown actually falls very close at -22.4%, but a Sharpe ratio of 1.48 nicely outperforms the 1.15 exhbited by the logistical regression model. At initial glance and analysis, I would think it would be safe to say that at least based on these preliminary statistics, the CNN model might show more promise for model performance when compared to the logistical regression model.

At least for AMZN, during the specific time interval we tested the dataset on. Again, if we change the time interval, and even the ticker to other stock, results for these models when compared side by side can undoubtedly vary. This is why it is important to test these circumstances for different stocks at a time, along with different associated time frames. At least, in order to possibly best attain the highest conviction rates possible. Also, it is important to keep in mind that while we only tested 10% of the dataset's tail end for the logistical regression model, we tested 20% on the CNN model. Despite that though, at least for AMZN during the allotted time span, we have ample evidence to confidently confirm that our second CNN neural network grossly outperformed the logistical regression model. For future testing purposes, we can always compare both models on a basket of stocks, as opposed to only one name at a time, and apply multiple time filters in attempt to raise our conviction further for which model is more sincerely superior on a comparative basis.

FURTHER POTENTIAL RESOURCES & PATHS FOR MACHINE/DEEP LEARNING EXPLORATION

Throughout our initial research and artificial intelligence algorithm creation efforts, we have already been able to reveal quite a lot when it comes to employing both machine and deep learning perspectives to a financial market environment. The statistics behind our two models seemed to undoubtedly support the second CNN deep learning probabilistic approach over the initial logistical regression machine learning one. Can we quickly come to the conclusion that the CNN is a better overall long-term model? Well, probably not. To truly get closer to which model may outperform the other, I would think it would be best to first employ these models on hundreds of other stocks in a given portfolio (or even alternate markets), along with multiple time frames (i.e. hourly, weekly, monthly). Doing so would probably better allow us to diversify our perspective in terms of which models seem to adapt and conform best to which specific markets at given periods of time. However, to handle such a task manually would probably be more cumbersome than anything; which is partly why many fund managers and quant firms on Wall Street are now investing large amounts of capital towards 'super computers' and big data in hope of seeking out such results in a much faster and efficient time frame.

In terms of different types of both machine and deep learning models, we have only touched the tip of the iceberg through our research efforts and exploration for these technologies. For python specifically, scikit-learn offers multiple types of machine learning frameworks in addition to logistical regression; ones that if utilized properly, could possibly outperform both of our models. A few popular approaches through scikit-learn and machine learning for finance are revolved around support vector machines, linear regression, K Nearest Neighbors, Naïve Bayes, etc. For keras and deep learning, another very popular model gaining traction in finance in addition to CNN is referred to as long short term memory (LSTM). These models are a special type of recurrent neural networks (RNNs), capable of learning long-term dependencies amongst dependent and independent variables and are now beginning to be applied to multiple types of global financial markets for predictive purposes. In terms of model stacking through ensembles, one will quickly recognize that with so many different options out there, the possibilities of creating multiple types of models is almost endless. Despite that, having the undying determination to attempt to create the one model that simply conforms and adapts to different market conditions better than any other is for many quant traders and analysts in itself, significantly rewarding. After all, If such an objective is attained with high levels of predictive probability, the rewards that could lie around the corner for such a milestone in breakthrough and achievement will probably be immense.

And with that, we finally circle back to our initially proposed fundamental question. Is machine learning is in fact the best approach to take on a long-term scale for predictive purposes; such as that for stock prices? The debate is one that continues to grow amongst the global financial community. And with the recent advancements in artificial intelligence and computing power, will probably only intensify in the coming years. One thing is for certain though; whether you are one who believes in its proposed promise. or one who is sincerely skeptical, artificial intelligence and machine learning is definitely not going anywhere. In addition to the stock market, its technologies are now being heavily implemented in the auto industry, video gaming via virtual reality, and within multiple medical avenues as well. The promise it brings to us in terms of making our everyday lives more convenient, and efficient, is one that is gaining mass respect as our technologies, such as python, continue to evolve and improve.

When it comes to applying such technologies to finance in general, it will probably come down to one fundamental aspect of reason. And that is, in time, will these intelligence machines actually be able to outperform the traditional Wall Street fund managers? Many of whom have been able to consistently, and respectfully, beat the market on a consistent basis many consecutive years. If this is in fact a reality, then I would say that there is no question in my mind that we are likely on the brink of the largest technological revelation Wall Street has ever experienced. Given that machines and deep learning continues to gain ground through more reliable computers utilizing cloud and big data services. And after all is said and done, will these mathematically generated formulas be able to deliver on their rising hype for consistently beating the market? Well, in that regard, I think it would be fair to say that only time will tell.

PYTHON

PROGRAMMING:

A STEP BY STEP GUIDE FOR BEGINNERS

Leonard Eddison

of this document is not allowed unless with written permission from the publisher. All rights reserved.

The information provided herein is stated to be truthful and consistent, in that any liability, in terms of inattention or otherwise, by any usage or abuse of any policies, processes, or directions contained within is the solitary and utter responsibility of the recipient reader. Under no circumstances will any legal responsibility or blame be held against the publisher for any reparation, damages, or monetary loss due to the information herein, either directly or indirectly.

Respective authors own all copyrights not held by the publisher.

The information herein is offered for informational purposes solely and is universal as so. The presentation of the information is without contract or any type of guarantee assurance.

The trademarks that are used are without any consent, and the publication of the trademark is without permission or backing by the trademark owner. All trademarks and brands within this book are for clarifying purposes only and are the owned by the owners themselves, not affiliated with this document.

Introduction

Chances are, if you're viewing this page, you're new to Python.

You might even be new to Programming altogether. Either way, you have come to the right place and chosen the right language!

Python is an easy to learn programming language, and I hope this book will convince you to take in consideration using it for your future projects. It is a great language for either beginners who are approaching the programming world or if you are already a professional programmer.

You don't have to be an expert to comprehend this book due to the fact that it will explain Python and the basic programming functions through a simple step-by-step process. It is also appropriate for those who are approaching computer programming for the first time.

You don't need to have a particular OS in order to run Python because it works perfectly on every OS.

In the first chapters, we will discuss the importance of learning how to use Python, its pros and cons.

In the fourth chapter, we will go through the process to install Python on Windows, Mac, and Linux.

From the fifth chapter, we will start a step-by-step process designed to take you from a pure beginner, who is approaching the programming world, to a student ready to start more complex projects.

I hope you enjoy this book...

CHAPTER ONE: I WANT TO START PROGRAMMING

Python is a powerful, high-level, object-oriented programming language created by Guido van Rossum.

It has simple, easy-to-use syntax, making it the perfect language for someone who is trying to learn computer programming for the first time.

This is a comprehensive guide on how to get started in Python, why you should learn it, and how you can learn it.

What is Python? - The Basics

Before getting started, let's get familiarized with the language.

Python is a general-purpose language. It has a wide range of applications from Web development (like: Django and Bottle), scientific and mathematical computing (Orange, SymPy, NumPy) to desktop graphical user Interfaces (Pygame, Panda3D).

The syntax of the language is clean, and the length of the code is relatively short. It's fun to work in Python because it allows you to think about the problem rather than focus on the syntax.

3 Reasons to Choose Python as First Language

-Simple Elegant Syntax

Programming in Python is fun. It's easier to understand and write Python code. Why? The syntax feels natural. Take this source code for example:

```
a = 2
b = 3
Sum = a + b
Print (sum)
```

Even if you have never programmed before, you can easily guess that this program adds two numbers and prints it.

Not overly strict

You don't need to define the type of variable in Python. Also, it's not necessary to add a semicolon at the end of the statement.

Python enforces you to follow good practices (like proper indentation). These small things can make learning much easier for beginners.

Great community and Support

Python has a large supporting community. There are numerous active forums online, which can be handy if you are stuck.

CHAPTER TWO: PROS AND CONS OF LEANING PYTHON

Python is a high-level, interpreted, and general-purpose dynamic programming language that focuses on code readability. The syntax in Python helps the programmers code in fewer steps compared to Java or C++.

Python is widely used in big companies because of its multiple programming paradigms. They usually involve imperative and object-oriented functional programs. It has a comprehensive and large standard library that has automatic memory management and dynamic features.

Why Companies Prefer Python?

Python has topped the charts in recent years over other programming languages like C, C++, and Java and is widely used by programmers. The language has undergone a drastic change since its release 25 years ago as many add-on features are introduced. The Python 1.0 had the module system of Modula-3 and interacted with Amoeba Operating System with varied functioning tools. Python 2.0, introduced in the year 2000, had the features of garbage collector and Unicode Support. Python 3.0, introduced in the year 2009, had a constructive design that avoids duplicate modules and constructs. With the added features, now companies are using Python 3.5.

Software development companies prefer the Python language because of its versatile features and fewer programming codes. Nearly 14% of programmers use it on operating systems like UNIX, Linux, Windows, and Mac OS. The programmers in big companies use Python as it has created a mark for itself in software development with characteristic features like-

- Interactive
- Interpreted
- Modular
- Dynamic
- Object-oriented
- Portable
- High level
- Extensible in C++ & C

- <u>Advantages or Benefits of Python</u>

The Python language has multiple applications in software development companies, such as in gaming, web frameworks and applications, language development, prototyping, graphic design applications etc. This provides the language with a higher plethora of advantages than other programming languages used in the industry. Some of its advantages are:

- Extensive Support Libraries

It provides a large standard library that includes areas like string operations, Internet, web service tools, operating system interfaces, and protocols. Most of the highly used programming tasks are already scripted into it, which limits the length of codes you need to write in Python.

- Integration Feature

Python integrates the Enterprise Application, making it easy to develop Web services by invoking COM or COBRA components. It has powerful control capabilities as it calls directly through C, C++, or Java via Jython. Python also processes XML and other markup languages as it can run on all modern operating systems through the same byte code.

- Improved Programmer's Productivity

The language has extensive support libraries and clean object-oriented designs that increase programmers' productivity by two to ten fold while using languages like Java, VB, Perl, C, C++ and C#.

- Productivity

Its strong process integration features, unit testing framework, and enhanced control capabilities contribute to the increased speed for most applications and productivity. It is a great option to build a scalable multi-protocol network application.

Limitations or Disadvantages of Python

Python has varied advantageous features, and programmers prefer this language to other programming languages because it is easy to learn and code. However, this language has still not made its place in some computing areas, including Enterprise Development Shops. Therefore, this language may not solve some of the enterprise solutions, and some limitations are:

- **Difficulty Using Other Languages**

Python lovers become so accustomed to its features and its extensive libraries that they face problems when learning or working on other programming languages. Python experts may see the declaring of cast "values" or variable "types", syntactic requirements of adding curly braces or semi colons as an onerous task.

- **Weak in Mobile Computing**

Python has made its presence on many desktop and server platforms, but it is seen as a weak language for mobile computing. This is the reason few mobile applications, like Carbonnelle, are built in it.

- **Slow Speed**

Python runs with the help of an interpreter instead of the compiler, which causes it to slow down because of the compilation and the execution that helps it to work normally. On the other hand, it can be seen that it is fast for many web applications.

- **Run-time Errors**

The Python language is dynamically typed so it has many design restrictions reported by some Python developers. It is even seen that it requires more testing time, and the errors always show up when the applications are finally run.

- **Underdeveloped Database Access Layers**

As compared to popular technologies, like JDBC and ODBC, Python's database access layer is found to be a bit underdeveloped and primitive. However, it cannot be applied in enterprises that need smooth interaction of complex legacy data.

PCAP: Programming Essentials in Python

Python is a general-purpose programming language used to build just about anything. Python is key for backend web development, data analysis, artificial intelligence, and scientific computing, all of which are key for pursuing IT careers. With PCAP: Programming Essentials in Python, you learn to design, write, debug, and run programs encoded in the Python language. No prior programming knowledge is required. The course begins with the very basics, guiding you step by step until you become adept at solving more complex problems. The course aligns to the PCAP – Python Certified Associate Programmer certification, validating your expertise to employers and expanding your IT and IoT career opportunities.

- Develop a working knowledge for how computers operate and how computer programs are executed.
- Evolve critical thinking and problem-solving skills using an algorithmic approach.
- Learn about the programmer's role in the software development process.
- Translate real-world issues into computer-solvable problems.
- Connect with the global Cisco Networking Academy community.

CHAPTER THREE: HOW TO INSTALL PYTHON (Windows, Mac and Linux)

In order to install Python, first, we need to download the right version for our OS.

The process is well-explained on www.python.org (the official website), where we will find the most suitable version for us. For that reason, we will keep the process explanation as short as possible.

Windows

In order to install Python on Windows, you first have to check the official site and click the voice download that you will find on the main menu.

At that point, you will see a page from which you can download your desired version of Python.

The process to download and install the program is very well-explained and straightforward.

From the moment the download is complete, we can start to write our first code:

Let's try with the simplest directive you can write: the "print" directive.

With this particular directive, the program will simply print out a line.

For this example, we will use the words "Let's start"

The code will appear like this:

```
print("Let's start")
Let's start
```

Linux

Chances are, if you own a computer that uses Linux, you will find python already installed. To verify it, just try to look for "Python" between your programs.

If you don't already have Python installed, you can download Python starting from the source code.

We'll get into that later.

Mac OS X

It's likely that you already have Python installed on this OS. Again, to verify it, you can look for the word "Python" in your Mac.

If you can't find Python on your device, you can easily download it from the site, using the .dmg format (disk image).

Source code

We need to choose our desired version of the program from the website before beginning to complete the source code.

Once you find the paragraph "All others", you will obtain the link that recalls the Source code for your version (example: Python - 3.0 . tgz.).

After we download the file, we need to extract the files in it. The tgz. format should be well-known to Linux and Mac users.

Searching on Google for the tgz and windows strings, we can get the utility to extract the format.

Once you do that, you should be able to run Python like any other program.

CHAPTER FOUR: INTERPRETER, INTERACTIVE

For most programming languages, you need to write the source code, compiling, and sometimes link the libraries in order to run the program.

With Python, everything is easier due to the fact that it allows you to run the source code directly (that is why it is defined as **Interpreter**) or even to write the instructions straight from its command prompt without creating or editing a source file **(Interactive).**

Sure, this last feature could seem a little odd, but we will see that, starting from the bottom, to try some new features or to test small parts from the your program, this feature is extremely fast and useful.

With the Interactive mode, you can easily play around and experiment with new syntax variations.

CHAPTER FIVE: PYTHON or PERL

Both Python and Perl are mature, open source, general purpose, high level, and interpreted programming languages. But the usage statistics posted on various websites depict that Python is currently more popular than Perl. Hence, a software developer can enhance his career prospects by switching from Perl to Python.

A beginner can further learn and use the Python programming language without putting extra time and effort. However, you must not switch to a new programming language just because of its popularity and usage. You must keep in mind the major differences between the two programming languages while deciding about migrating from Perl to Python.

12 Points You Must Keep in Mind while Switching from Perl to Python

1) Design Goal

Perl was originally designed as a scripting language to simplify report processing capabilities. It comes with built-in text processing capability. On the other hand, Python was designed initially as a hobby programming language. But it was designed with features to help programmers build applications with concise, readable, and reusable code. The two programming languages still differ in the categories of features and performance.

2) Syntax Rules

The syntax rules of both Python and Perl are influenced by several other programming languages.

97

For instance, Perl borrows features from a number of programming languages, including C, shell script, sed, AWK, and Lisp. Likewise, Python implements functional programming features in a manner similar to Lisp. In addition to being easy to use, the Python syntax rules further enable programmers to except many concepts with less and readable code.

3) Family of Languages

Perl belongs to a family of high-level programming languages that includes Perl 5 and Perl 6. The versions 5 and 6 of Perl are compatible with each other. A developer can easily migrate from Perl 5 to Perl 6 without putting extra time and effort. The different versions of Python are not compatible with each other. Hence, a programmer has to choose from two distinct versions of the programming language.

4) Ways to Achieve Same Results

Python enables programmers to express concepts without writing long lines of code. But it requires programmers to accomplish tasks or achieve results in a specific and single way. On the other hand, Perl enables programmers to accomplish a single task or achieve the same results in a number of ways. Hence, many programmers find Perl to be more flexible than Python, but the multiple ways to achieve the same result often make the code written in Perl messy and the application difficult to maintain.

5) Web Scripting Language

Perl was originally designed as a UNIX scripting language. Many developers use Perl as a scripting language to avail its built-in text processing capabilities. However, there are many web developers who complain that Perl is slower than other widely used scripting languages. Python is also used widely by programmers for web application development. But it lacks built-in web development capabilities. Hence, developers have to avail various frameworks and tools to write web applications in Python efficiently and rapidly.

6) Web Application Frameworks

Most developers nowadays avail the tools and features provided by various frameworks to build web applications efficiently and rapidly. Perl web programmers have options to choose from an array of frameworks, including Catalyst, Dancer, Mojolicious, Poet, Interchange, Jifty, and Gantry. Likewise, the web developers have the option to use a number of Python web frameworks, including Django, Flask, Pyramid, Bottle, and Cherrypy. However, the number of Python web frameworks is much higher than the number of Perl web frameworks.

7) Usage

As mentioned earlier, both Python and Perl are general-purpose programming languages. Hence, each programming language is used to develop a variety of software applications. Perl is used widely for graphic and network programming, system administration, and development of finance and biometric applications, whereas Python comes with a robust standard library that simplifies web application development, scientific computing, big data solution development, and artificial intelligence tasks. Hence, developers prefer using Python for development of advanced and mission-critical software applications.

8) Performance and Speed

A number of studies have shown that Python is slower than other programming languages, like

Java and C++. Developers frequently explore ways to enhance the execution speed of Python code. Someone even replaced default Python runtime with their own custom runtime to make the Python applications run faster. Many programmers find Perl to be faster than Python. Many web developers use Perl as a scripting language to make web applications faster and deliver enhanced user experience.

9) Structured Data Analysis

At the moment, big data is one of the hottest trends in software development. Many enterprises nowadays build custom applications for collecting, storing, and analyzing a huge amount of structured and unstructured data. The PDL provided by Perl enables developers to analyze big data. The built-in text processing capability of Perl further simplifies and speeds up analysis of a huge amount of structured data. But Python is used widely by programmers for data analysis. The developers further take advantage of robust Python libraries, like Numpy, to process and analyze huge volumes of data in a faster and more efficient way.

10) JVM Interoperability

At the moment, Java is one of the programming languages used widely for development of desktop, web, and mobile applications. In comparison to Perl, Python interoperates with Java Virtual Machine (JVM) seamlessly and efficiently. Hence, the developers have the option to write Python code that runs smoothly on JVM, while taking advantage of robust Java APIs and objects. The interoperability helps programmers to build application by targeting the popular Java platform while writing code in Python instead of Java.

11) Advanced Object Oriented Programming

Both Perl and Python are object-oriented programming languages. But Python implements advanced object oriented programming languages in a better way than Perl. While writing code in Perl, programmers still need to use packages instead of classes. Many developers find it difficult to keep the code simple and readable while writing object oriented code in Perl. But Perl makes it easier for programmers to accomplish a variety of tasks simply by using one liners on the command line.

12) Text Processing Capability

Unlike Python, Perl was designed with built-in text processing capabilities. Hence, many programmers prefer using Perl for report generation. Perl further makes it easier for programmers to perform regex and string comparison operations, like matching, replacement, and substitution. It does not require developers to write additional code to perform exception handling and I/O operations.

Hence, many programmers prefer Perl to Python when they have to build applications to process textual data or generate reports.

CHAPTER SIX: OBJECT ORIENTED

We won't get into this expression in detail, (a universally accepted definition still doesn't exist). What we can say about this paradigm is that it means to think about the problem solution, not as a succession of instructions, but as objects and its respective attributes.

Python programmers can write high quality and modular code by using classes and objects.

With an object oriented language, we can face the problem with a different approach. For instance, we can define an object, give it a name, and from that moment, we can forget the definition due to the fact that it has been already saved.

Furthermore, we can save the physical state inside the file in order to open it only once. By doing so, our object will give us all the reading and writing functions we need.

Let's take an example of Class

```
>>> class fruit:
"""        tipo = "vegetable"
"""

>>> apple = fruit ()
>>> print apple.tipo
Vegetable
>>>
```

CHAPTER SEVEN: MODULES

In order to use a programming language, you often need to import several libraries that you will need in order to find codes.

A Python users' life is simplified due to the fact that you can find a ton of tested and functioning libraries.

Libraries in Python are called "modules".

"Modules" are pre-written Python codes that you "import" in your Python program. Since there are many tasks that people commonly do, we have modules that people have written that do these tasks for you, and they usually do them in the cleanest and most efficient way possible. Sometimes, you will see people refer to "DRY." This stands for Don't Repeat Yourself, which often also translates into "Don't Repeat Someone Else."

The phrase "wrapper" means that someone has placed, like a wrapper, Python code over another language. So, when you have a Python wrapper around a C++ code, what someone has done is written some Python code that interacts with the C++ language. This allows you to make use of various aspects of the language being wrapped, in this case C++, without actually needing to know or understand that language.

Thus, Python can be used to make games, do data analysis, control robot and hardware, create GUIs, or even to create websites.

"GUI" stands for Graphical User Interface and is used to describe a program that incorporates graphics to make the program more interactive for the user.

Now, let's see how to import a library on Python.

You can gain access to a module by simply using the "import" statement. Doing this, you will execute the code of the module.

In order to have access to a module, the user must first look for a built-in module in Python (Python has a wide variety of build-in functions that allow the user to start its journey in programming; if the user wants to experiment with different functions, he/she may need to import a module). If the corresponding module is not already built in, we need to import it.

Let's see a practical example:

Let's say that I want to import a module called "example1".

I'll run the statement for that module:

Import example1

And it's as easy as that.

CHAPTER EIGHT: LET'S DIVE IN

Now, we will dive into Python, discovering the various commands, lists, strings, and so on...

IDLE

You will find "IDLE" (Integrated Development Environment) in the main menu, and it will allow you to edit, run, and test the codes that you will create.

IDLE has the following features:

coded in Python, using the tkinter GUI toolkit

cross-platform: It has the same features whether you're using Windows, Unix, Mac OS X, or Linux

Python shell window (interactive interpreter) with colorizing of code input, output, and error messages

multi-window text editor with multiple undo, Python colorizing, smart indent, call tips, auto completion, and other features

search within any window, replace within editor windows, and search through multiple files (grep) debugger with persistent breakpoints, stepping, and viewing of global and local namespaces configuration, browsers, and other dialogs

IDLE has two main window types: The first one is the Shell window, and the second is the Editor window. You can easily run multiple editor windows at the same time. Output windows are a subtype of edit window. They currently have the same top menu as the Editor windows but a different default title and context menu.

IDLE's menus change dynamically based on which window is currently selected.

Each menu documented below indicates which window type it is associated with.

Now, let's run IDLE and digit the command we already tried.

print("Let's start")

We can see how the program processes our command.

Since we don't want to digit the codes every time, we will now save the source code.

EDITING

Let's run the command File/New window that we will find in the IDLE menu, and we will open a new window without the command prompt.

In this new window, we will write our beloved code once again:

print("Let's start")

But this time, we click on the "file/save", and we save our file, naming it start.py in a directory.

Now, we can run our newly created program from IDLE with the command "run".

There are a lot of editors available to write Python programs. Let's see the most famous:

- Eclipse with PyDev: Eclipse has a massive community of developers, and it allows you a great level of customization.

- Eric: Eric writes in Python using qt framework, and it utilizes Scintilla, which is a source code editing component.

- PyCharm: It has its own free community, which is definitely useful when you're learning to code.

- Other good options may be: PyScripter, LeoEditor, Bluefish, Ptk, Spyder, and Geany.

CHAPTER NINE: VARIOUS TYPES OF DATA

Luckily for us, Python has a good set of built-in functions that perform very well especially for beginners.

We will now learn the main built-in function:

1.   **The type function**: It returns the datatype of any arbitrary object. The type function can even take a variable and return it as datatype. You can use this function to compare different types of objects.

Let's see an example:

n=1

type(n)

<type 'int'>

S=start

<type 'str'>

import smtplib

type (smtplib)

2. **The dir Command**: The syntax of dir in the following: dir([object]), dir allows us to obtain a list of valid attributes for a given object.

Let's see a practical example of how dir works:

class Person:

```
def __dir__(self):
    return ['age', 'gender', 'salary']
```

```
carpenter = Person()
print(dir(carpenter))
```

This command will appear like this once you run it:

```
['age', 'gender', 'salary']
```

3. **List**: (Syntax: list([iterable)]) this command has the purpose of creating a list whose items are the same and in the same order as *iterable*'s items; *iterable* may be either a sequence, a container that supports iteration, or an iterator object.

Let's now see a simple list:

```
list = [2, 6 , 12]
list
```

Let's run the command, and the result will be the following:

```
2, 6, 12
```

In order to use values in lists, we can use the square brackets. Hhere's an example:

```
list1 = ['math', 'history', 1993, 1994];
list2 = [1, 2, 3, 4, 5, 6, 7 ];
print "list1[0]: ", list1[0]
print "list2[1:5]: ", list2[1:5]
```

Once we run it, we will have the following output:

list1[0]: math

list2[1:5]: [2, 3, 4, 5]

lists can be updated using the command append()

I'll give you an example:


```
list = ['math', 'history', 1993, 1994];
print "Value available at index 2 : "
print list[2]
list[2] = 1995;
print "New value available at index 2 : "
print list[2]
```


And the output will be the following:

Value available at index 2 :

1993

New value available at index 2 :

1995

We can also delete elements:

list1 = ['math', 'history', 1993, 1994];

print list1

del list1[2];

print "After deleting value at index 2 : "

print list1

With the following output:

['math', 'history', 1993, 1994]

After deleting value at index 2 :

['math', 'history', 1994]

There are some expressions that we can use with lists:

Length: len([1, 2, 3]) → 3

Concatenation: [1, 2, 3] + [4, 5, 6] → [1, 2, 3, 4, 5, 6]

Repetition: ['Let's start'] * 3 → ['Let's start', 'Let's start', 'Let's start']

Membership: 3 in [1, 2, 3] → True

In regard to list's built-in functions, I'll list the most important:

- cmp(list1, list2) → compares elements of both lists
- len(list) → gives the total length of the list
- max(list) → returns item from the list with max value
- min(list) → returns item from the list with min valuw
- list(seq) → converts a tuple into list (we'll see what a tuple is in a moment)

In regard to list's built-in methods, I'll list the most important:

- list.append(obj) → Appends object obj to list
- list.count(obj) → Returns count of how many times obj occurs in list
- list.extend(seq) → Appends the contents of seq to list
- list.index(obj) → Returns the lowest index in list that obj appears

- list.insert(index, obj) → Inserts object obj into list at offset index
- list.pop(obj=list[-1]) → Removes and returns last object or obj from list
- list.remove(obj) → Removes object obj from list
- list.reverse() → reverses objects of list in place
- list.sort([func]) → Sorts objects of list, use compare func if given

4. **Strings**: Strings in Python have a lot of interesting features. They are immutable (after you create a string, you cannot modify it), and if you need a new string, you can simply create it.

So, in the expression ('let's' + 'start'), we will have a new string composed of the two strings 'let's' and 'start'.

Let's see a practical example:

s = 'let's'

```
print s [1]          ## i
print len(s)         ##2
print s + ' start '    ## let's start
```

Now, let's see a couple of examples of strings using the *slicing* function.

```
s = "0123456789"
```

With the following function:

```
s [:5]
```

You can select the first 5 numbers

```
'01234'
```

With the following function:

```
s [-5:]
```

you can select the last 5 numbers

```
'56789'
```

Keep in mind that Python uses zero-based indexing; therefore, if str is 'hello' str[1] is 'e'.

In order to wrap, we need to utilize the backslash followed by "n". Let's see an example:

```
s = "8\n9\n10\nHi"

print s

8
```

9

10

HI

The "\n" character is a special one. Here is a list of the most important special characters:

1.   "\t" is a tab

2.   "\r" is a carriage return

3.   "\\" is the literal backslash character.

4.   "\b" is the backspace

We can use the "+" symbol to join two strings:

s = ex

p = ample

s + p

'example'

Or we can multiply a string using the "*" symbol:

s = example

s * 5

'exampleexampleexampleexampleexample'

In Python, we can find a lot of string methods (a method is similar to a function that runs on an object). We will now take a look at the most commonly used:

- s.lower(), s.upper() -- returns the lowercase or uppercase version of the string

- s.strip() -- returns a string with whitespace removed from the start and end

- s.isalpha()/s.isdigit()/s.isspace()... -- tests if all the string chars are in the various character classes

- s.startswith('other'), s.endswith('other') -- tests if the string starts or ends with the given other string

- s.find('other') -- searches for the given other string (not a regular expression) within s and returns the first index where it begins or -1 if not found

- s.replace('old', 'new') -- returns a string where all occurrences of 'old' have been replaced by 'new'

- s.split('delim') -- returns a list of substrings separated by the given delimiter. The delimiter is not a regular expression. It's just text.

- 'aaa,bbb,ccc'.split(',') -> ['aaa', 'bbb', 'ccc']. As a convenient special case s.split() (with no arguments) splits on all whitespace chars.

- s.join(list) -- opposite of split(), joins the elements in the given list using the string as the delimiter. e.g. '---'.join(['aaa', 'bbb', 'ccc']) -> aaa---bbb---ccc

5. Tuples

With the term "tuple", we are referring to a sequence of objects that are immutable in Python.

If a tuple is empty, it will appear as the following:

```
tup1 = ()
```

If a tuple includes even only one value, we have to include a comma:

```
tup1 = (1,)
```

Let's see some more tuples:

```
tup1 = ('dog', 'cat', 'fish', 'seal' )
tup2 = (1, 2, 3, 4 )
```

Tuples can be sliced, concatenated and more, just like strings, but in order to do that, we have to use square brackets:

```
tup1 = ('dog', 'cat', 'fish', 'seal')
tup2 = (1, 2, 3, 4 )
```

```
print "tup1[0]: ", tup1[0]
print "tup2[1:4]: ", tup2[2:3]
```

Once we execute this code, we will have this result:

```
tup1[0]: dog
tup2[1:4]: (3,)
```

If you were expecting a different output that is because tuples indices begin at 0.

As already said, tuples are immutable. If you need to add or delete elements, you have to create a new tuple. Let's see an example:

At first, we will look at how we can create a new tuple with the desired elements:

```
tup1 = (1, 2, 3)
tup2 = ('dog', 'cat', 'fish')
tup3 = tup1 + tup2
```

Now, we just have to run the print command, and this will be the result:

```
print (tup3)
```

(1, 2, 3, 'dog', 'cat', 'fish')

Lists and tuples are similar. The main difference is that, while lists can be modified at any time, tuples are immutable. Moreover, while tuples use parentheses, lists use square brackets.

Tuples, just like lists, respond to any general operation, like those we have seen in the chapter regarding lists (length, concatenation, repetition, membership and iteration).

We can find built-in functions also for tuples:

- cmp(tuple1, tuple2) → Compares elements of both tuples.
- len(tuple) → Gives the total length of the tuple.
- max(tuple) → Returns item from the tuple with max value.
- min(tuple) → Returns item from the tuple with

- min value tuple(seq) → Converts a list into tuple.

6.   Sets

A set is a type of data that allows us to handle groups of elements. It creates a collection of unordered and unique elements. Set objects also support mathematical operations like union, intersection, difference, and symmetric difference.

Let's see an example:

a = set ('example')

b = set ('exile')

- a

{ 'e', 'x', 'a', 'm', 'p', 'l'}

As you can see, this set is missing the last "e", and that is because, as we said before, sets only contain unique elements.

But let's continue with our example:

- a – b (with this function, we can build a set formed only by the letters in a but not the letters in b)

{ 'a', 'm', 'p'}

- a | b (it takes the letters in a and in b)

{ 'e', 'x', 'a', 'm', 'p', 'l', 'i'}

- a & b (it takes the letters contained in both a and b)

{ 'e', 'x', 'l'}

- a ^ b (it takes the letters in a or in b but not in both)

{ 'a', 'm', 'p', 'l'}

Sets don't support indexing and slicing

In order to add elements, we will have to use the add() command for a single element and the update() command for multiple elements.

In order to remove elements, we will have to use discard() or remove(), whereas if we need to remove all the elements in the set, we can use clear().

Sets are useful to carry out mathematical operations. Let's see an example:

A = {1, 2, 3, 4, 5}

B = {4, 5, 6, 7, 8}

Now, there are 4 possible operations: union, intersection, difference, and symmetric difference. Let's see them in action:

1. Union: For this operation, we can use | operator or the method union()

```
# initialize A and B
A = {1, 2, 3, 4, 5}
B = {4, 5, 6, 7, 8}


# use | operator
# Output: {1, 2, 3, 4, 5, 6, 7, 8}
print(A | B)
```

2. Intersection: This operation will include the elements that are common in both sets, and we will use the method intersection():

```
# initialize A and B
A = {1, 2, 3, 4, 5}
B = {4, 5, 6, 7, 8}


# use & operator
```

Output: {4, 5}

print(A & B)

3.	Difference: With this operation, we can have the elements that appear in A but not in B or vice versa. It is performed using the method difference ():

initialize A and B

A = {1, 2, 3, 4, 5}

B = {4, 5, 6, 7, 8}

use - operator on A

Output: {1, 2, 3}

print(A – B)

4.	Symmetric difference: This operation allows us to take the elements in both A and B, leaving aside those that appear in both. It is done through the method symmetric_difference():

initialize A and B

A = {1, 2, 3, 4, 5}

B = {4, 5, 6, 7, 8}

```
# use ^ operator
# Output: {1, 2, 3, 6, 7, 8}
print(A ^ B)
```

In Python, we can find a list of built-in methods for sets. I will list the most useful:

- add() → Add an element to a set
- clear() → Remove all elements from a set
- copy() → Return a shallow copy of a set
- difference() → Return the difference of two or more sets as a new set
- difference_update() → Remove all elements of another set from this set
- discard() → Remove an element from set if it is a member. (Do nothing if the element is not in set)
- intersection() → Return the intersection of two sets as a new set
- intersection_update() → Update the set with the intersection of itself and another

- isdisjoint() → Return True if two sets have a null intersection
- issubset() → Return True if another set contains this set
- issuperset() → Return True if this set contains another set
- pop() → Remove and return an arbitary set element. Raise KeyError if the set is empty
- remove() → Remove an element from a set. If the element is not a member, raise a KeyError
- symmetric_difference() → Return the symmetric difference of two sets as a new set
- symmetric_difference_update() → Update a set with the symmetric difference of itself and another
- union() → Return the union of sets in a new set
- update() → Update a set with the union of itself and others

- In Python, we can also find a list of built-in functions:

- all() Return True if all elements of the set are true (or if the set is empty).

- any() Return True if any element of the set is true. If the set is empty, return False.

- enumerate() Return an enumerate object. It contains the index and value of all the items of set as a pair.

- len() Return the length (the number of items) in the set. max() Return the largest item in the set.

- min() Return the smallest item in the set.

- sorted() Return a new sorted list from elements in the set(does not sort the set itself).

- sum() Retrun the sum of all elements in the set.

7.   dictionaries

Python has a built-in function, called the dictionary, which massively simplifies our work.

The dictionary is a set of keys, and we can extract the set of values given by it.

In order to build a dictionary, we can utilize the constructor dict(). Let's see it in action:

```
rooms = dict ()
rooms[ 'guest1' ] = '101'
rooms [ 'guest2' ] = '102'
```

The dictionary we just built will be like this:

Rooms

{ 'guest1' : '101' , 'guest2' : '102' }

We can easily extract and add new elements to our dictionary using the key method

```
Rooms.keys()
[ 'guest1', 'guest2' ]
```

Other interesting functions are: has_key (useful to determine if an element is in the dictionary), del (useful to delete an element), clear, copy, fromkey, get, items, and so on...

Dictionaries in Python have many built-in methods. As usual, I'll list the most useful:

- clear() Remove all items from the dictionary.
- copy() Return a shallow copy of the dictionary.
- fromkeys(seq[, v]) Return a new dictionary with keys from seq and value equal to v (defaults to None).
- get(key[,d]) Return the value of key. If key does not exist, return d (defaults to None).
- items() Return a new view of the dictionary's items (key, value).
- keys() Return a new view of the dictionary's keys.
- pop(key[,d]) Remove the item with key and return its value or d if key is not found. If d is not provided and key is not found, raises KeyError.
- popitem() Remove and return an arbitary item (key, value). Raises KeyError if the dictionary is empty.

- setdefault(key[,d]) If key is in the dictionary, return its value. If not, insert key with a value of d and return d (defaults to None).

- update([other]) Update the dictionary with the key/value pairs from other, overwriting existing keys.

- values() Return a new view of the dictionary's values.

8. True, false and none

False and none are two constant objects in Python, referred to as Boolean values.

Python has a built-in function bool () that can be used to transform any value to a Boolean and check if the value can be interpreted as true or false.

Let's see an example:

odd_numbers = (1, 2, 3, 4, 5, 6)

x = 2 in odd numbers

x

false

y = 4 in even_numbers

y = true

If an element has a "none value", it means that it lacks a precise value.

9. Conversions

Python has some built-in function that allow you to convert elements. Here you can see how:

tuple(l) → to convert a list to a tuple

list(t) → to convert a tuple to a list

CHAPTER TEN: SYNTAX

We have just gotten in touch with the various types of data in Python. Now, we should find out which commands can be used.

First, we will look into the indentation; second, we will explain the control flow statements – if, for, while, break, continue, and pass.

Indentation

The indentation is one of the most characterizing syntactic elements of Python.

Let's see a classic example:

```python
def perm(l):
        # Compute the list of all permutations of l
    if len(l) <= 1:
            return [l]
    r = []
    for i in range(len(l)):
```

```
s = l[:i] + l[i+1:]
p = perm(s)
for x in p:
  r.append(l[i:i+1] + x)
return r
```

As you can see, it is easy to see where the code ends and where the following code line starts.

The indentation is used to indicate a block of code. Obviously you must indent each block with the same amount of spaces. In Python, we use indentations to indicate to what block a particular string of code belongs.

Another great feature is that the universal block closing rules are universal, so we do not need to specify *end, endif, fi,* parentheses or brackets, *wend, endwhile, next, loop, end procedure or end function.* We only need to respect the *indentation.*

The IF statement

What is a *Control Flow Statement*? It's a feature that allows the program to take decisions, depending on the situation, reading the code in a particular order. We can control the statement execution using some control flow tools.

The IF instruction is probably the most used command among all programming languages.

We can use IF to check a condition.

Here is an example of how IF works:

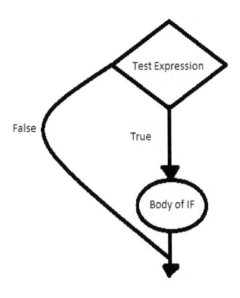

We run a block of statement only if the condition IF is true; otherwise, we operate another statement.

Example of IF statement syntax:

x = int(input("Please enter an integer: "))
Please enter an integer: 42

```
if x < 0:
x = 0
print('Negative changed to zero')
 elif x == 0:
print('Zero')
elif x == 1:
print ('Single')
 else:
print('more')
```

More

We can observe ":" that we used to end the test that controls the program flow.

You can insert as many *Elif as* you need; in the example above, the last Elif is not obligatory.

The FOR statement

The For instruction allows us to define iterations. To decide how many iterations we need and on which element we have to perform the iteration, we must use any object we can consider sequence.

Traditionally used to repeat a string of code an exact number of times.

We have already seen many sequence examples: lists, tuple, strings. These are all data we can use to iterate with For:

```
for c in "abc":
Print c
A
B
C
>>>
```

How can we execute a simple iteration a certain number of times without having the right sequence?

We could use "range"

for n range (4):

Print n

1

2

3

4

>>>

*With the command "range", we can also choose the start and the end of an iteration.

"For" allows us also to execute a cycle on more variables at the same time.

This is possible due to the fact that the "items" method in a dictionary gives a list of *tuples* composed by their own key and value.

"For" establishes a cycle on every element in this list and gives to the variables *key* and *value* the values we have in each *tuple.*

The WHILE statement

The *While* instruction is similar to the *For* instruction. The only difference is that the iteration is not based on a fixed sequence but executes the operation as long as the given condition is true.

Here is an example of how While works:

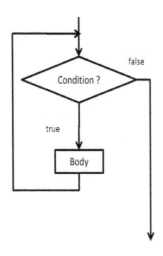

x = 1

while x < 7:

147

```
Print x

X += 1

1

2

3

4

5

6

>>>
```

In the example above, (the increment statement), is executed until the count remains below 7.

If a condition remains True, we have a so-called "Infinite Loop". In that case, you should press CTRL + C to close the program.

The Break and Continue

Break and Continue are used to stop an iteration to pass to the next one.

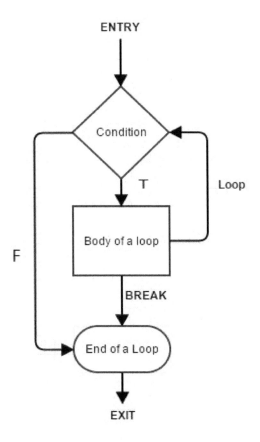

You will often use *Break* in *for loop* and *while loop* as in these classic examples*:*

For var in sequence:

```
# codes inside for loop
If condition:
    Break
# codes inside for loop
#codes outside for loop
```

```
While test expression:
# codes inside while loop
If condition:
    Break
# codes inside the loop
# codes outside while loop
```

Now that we have gotten in touch with the instructions *break* and *continue,* let's step back to *for* and *while* because they have another peculiarity, the instruction: *Else.*

It was an *If* clause, but *"else"* is also very useful with cycles due to the fact that all the instructions we will write in *else* will be executed at the cycle end (if we do not end the cycle first with a *break).*

Example of if – else

Num = 8

If num >= 5:

Print("positive or zero")

Else

Print("negative number")

*try with different numbers as well

With this program, you can check if the number is positive, negative, or zero.

CHAPTER ELEVEN: FUNCTIONS

What is a function?

It is a block of code used to perform a specific task.

Through *Functions,* we can break our program. This allows us to have better modularity in favor of organization and better reusability.

We usually come across 3 different types of functions in Python:

1.   User-Defined Functions; functions created by the user

2.   Built-in Functions; (list below)

3.   Anonymous Functions; also known as Lambda Functions, are created in Python using a construction called "lambda".

Here is a list of: Built-in Functions

➤ Python abs()	➤ *returns absolute value of a number*
➤ Python any()	➤ *Checks if any Element of an Iterable is True*
➤ Python all()	➤ *returns true when all elements in iterable is true*
➤ Python ascii()	➤ *Returns String Containing Printable Representation*
➤ Python bin()	➤ *converts integer to binary string*
➤ Python bool()	➤ *Coverts a Value to Boolean*
➤ Python bytearray()	➤ *returns array of given byte size*
➤ Python callable()	➤ *Checks if the Object is Callable*
➤ Python	➤ *returns immutable bytes*

bytes()	*object*
➤ Python chr()	➤ *Returns a Character (a string) from an Integer*
➤ Python compile()	➤ *Returns a Python code object*
➤ Python classmethod()	➤ *returns class method for given function*
➤ Python complex()	➤ *Creates a Complex Number*
➤ Python delattr()	➤ *Deletes Attribute from the Object*
➤ Python dict()	➤ *Creates a Dictionary*
➤ Python dir()	➤ *Tries to Return Attributes of Object*
➤ Python divmod()	➤ *Returns a Tuple of Quotient and Remainder*

➤ Python enumerate()	➤ *Returns an Enumerate Object*
➤ Python staticmethod()	➤ *creates static method from a function*
➤ Python filter()	➤ *constructs iterator from elements which are true*
➤ Python eval()	➤ *Runs Python Code Within Program*
➤ Python float()	➤ *returns floating point number from number, string*
➤ Python format()	➤ *returns formatted representation of a value*
➤ Python frozenset()	➤ *returns immutable frozenset object*

➢ Python getattr()	➢ *returns value of named attribute of an object*
➢ Python globals()	➢ *returns dictionary of current global symbol table*
➢ Python exec()	➢ *Executes Dynamically Created Program*
➢ Python hasattr()	➢ *returns whether object has named attribute*
➢ Python help()	➢ *Invokes the built-in Help System*
➢ Python hex()	➢ *Converts to Integer to Hexadecimal*
➢ Python hash()	➢ *returns hash value of an object*
➢ Python input()	➢ *reads and returns a line of string*
➢ Python id()	➢ *Returns Identify of an Object*

➢ Python isinstance()	➢ *Checks if a Object is an Instance of Class*
➢ Python int()	➢ *returns integer from a numberor strings*
➢ Python issubcla ss()	➢ *Checks if a Object is Subclass of a Class*
➢ Python iter()	➢ *returns iterator for an object*
➢ Python list() Function	➢ *creates list in Python*
➢ Python locals()	➢ *returns dictionary of current local symbol table*
➢ Python len()	➢ *Returns Length of an Object*
	➢ *returns largest element*

➢ Python max()	
➢ Python min()	➢ *returns smallest element*
➢ Python map()	➢ *Applies Function and Returns a List*
➢ Python next()	➢ *Retrieves Next Element from Iterator*
➢ Python memory view()	➢ *returns memory view of an argument*
➢ Python object()	➢ *Creates a Featureless Object*
➢ Python oct()	➢ *converts integer to octal*
➢ Python ord()	➢ *returns Unicode code point for Unicode*

character

➢ Python open()	➢ *Returns a File object*
➢ Python pow()	➢ *returns x to the power of y*
➢ Python print()	➢ *Prints the Given Object*
➢ Python property ()	➢ *returns a property attribute*
➢ Python range()	➢ *return sequence of integers between start and stop*
➢ Python repr()	➢ *returns printable representation of an object*
	➢ *returns reversed iterator*

➢ Python reversed ()	*of a sequence*
➢ Python round()	➢ *rounds a floating point number to ndigits places.*
➢ Python set()	➢ *returns a Python set*
➢ Python setattr()	➢ *sets value of an attribute of object*
➢ Python slice()	➢ *creates a slice object specified by range()*
➢ Python sorted()	➢ *returns sorted list from a given iterable*
➢ Python str()	➢ *returns informal representation of an object*
➢ Python sum()	➢ *Add items of an Iterable*

➤ Python tuple() Function	➤ *Creates a Tuple*
➤ Python type()	➤ *Returns Type of an Object*
➤ Python vars()	➤ *Returns __dict__ attribute of a class*
➤ Python zip()	➤ *Returns an Iterator of Tuples*
➤ Python __import__()	➤ *Advanced Function Called by import*
➤ Python super()	➤ *Allow you to Refer Parent Class by super*

The instruction that allows us to create a function is *Def.*

Example:

Def fact (n):

    If n < 2:

Return 1

    Return n * fact (n − 1)

The function *Fact* accepts only one parameter, named "n". The *return* instruction is used to end the function giving back the right number.

As you can see in the last example, we can find:

•   The keyword *def* followed by the function name

•   An argument (n)

•   To mark the end of the function, we use a colon (:)

•   With the same indentation level, we write another valid statement to create the function body.

- A final *return* statement to exit the function.

Def functionname(parameters):

"function_docstring"

Function_suite

Return [expression]

Docstring: A *docstring* is used to explain what that function does. It is optional, but sometimes, you need to document what you're writing.

Return: The *return* statement is used to exit a function and hand back a value to its caller.

How do functions work in Python?

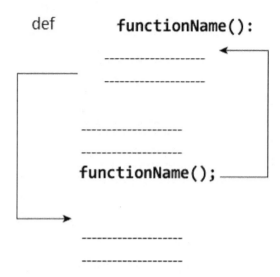

With a function, you can:

- Define the function

- Call a function

How to define a function

You can easily define a function using the keywords *def*, as previously shown, to declare a function. Subsequently, the programmer will add parameters (within parenthesis) to the function as well as statements to be executed to the function itself. At the end, insert the *return* statement to exit the function.

Call a function

What "calling a function means"

Calling a function is the process to execute the function you have defined. You can call a function either from the Python prompt or through other functions.

The return Statement

In the previous section, you have already seen the *return* statement. Basically, it gives something back or replies to the function caller (*print command* only produces text).

When a function ends without the *return* statement, it is the same as a *return None.*

All the below functions [F1, F2, F3] will give back a *None:*

```
def f1():
    pass
def f2():
    return
def f3():
    return None
```

We can also verify it in *IDLE:*

```
>>> print  f1(),  f2(),  f3()
None   None   None
>>>
```

CHAPTER TWELVE: CLASSES

Now that we've seen the types of data, syntax, and functions, we are going to merge them to learn to create new classes in Python.

First, we should define what a class is as well as what an object is:

An object is an encapsulation of variables and functions into a single entity. A class is a template that you can use to create objects.

The Classes provide objects with valiables and functions.

We can say that a class is a blueprint to create objects.

So, let's jump into that by creating our first class! First, we have to define a class with the *class operator*:

```
# Defining a class
class class_name:
```

167

[statement 1]

[statement 2]

[statement 3]

[etc.]

Now, we've created a new local namespace where we can define the attributes of the given class; attributes are data or functions.

We can access data and functions through the class objects that were authomatically created when we created our class.

In order to access attributes and to add new objects of a class, we have to use this class object.

Finally, we can create an object. The procedure is straight forward as usual:

ob = MyClass()

We just created a new instance object that we named ob.

Objects and attributes can be easily deleted using the del statement. Let's see an example:

c1 = ComplexNumber(1,3)

del c1

c1

Classes include methods. A method is basically a function that takes a class instance as its first parameter.

Let's make an example:

```
class movies:

"sub categories of movies"

def _init_(self, horror=0 ,

                thriller=0 ,

                drama=0) :

self.horror = horror

self.thriller = thriller

self.drama = drama
```

CHAPTER THIRTEEN: WHAT CAUSES FATAL ERRORS AND HOW TO FIX IT

If you encounter fatal exception errors whenever you use your PC, then you are probably wondering why it happens and what causes them. Basically, the fatal exception is an error message that many PC users encounter as they use their computers. This particular error will indicate that the program you are running and the one that caused the error will need to be closed.

The fatal exception error simply means the exception cannot be handled in order for the program to continue running.

You have to understand that software programs need to communicate with the operating system through layers of codes. When the operating system encounters an invalid code or an illegal software program instruction, it will usually result in the fatal exception error.

Generally, fatal exception errors are caused by incompatibility of the programs you try running. It can also be caused by improperly written programs, as well as hardware related issues, such as overheating of a specific hardware.

There are quite a lot of causes for fatal exception errors. So, here are some effective solutions that may solve this problem.

The first is by disabling any programs running that may cause a conflict between the programs that are already running and the programs that you try running. By disabling a particular program first, you will be able to prevent fatal exception errors.

You might also want to delete temporary files, as this is also a common cause for fatal exception errors.

Defragmenting the hard drive as well as running Scandisk will prevent data corruption, which is also a cause of fatal exception errors.

CHAPTER FOURTEEN: BEST PRACTICES FOR HANDLING WEBSITE ERRORS

This chapter explains the process of implementing error handling for a website that utilizes server-side scripting. Proper error handling is necessary to ensure that users of a website have a good experience during their visit. Any professional website should be thoroughly tested on a staging server before being deployed on the live web server. However, it is not always possible to anticipate every possible error, and good error handling will notify both the user and the webmaster about problems with the website in a production environment.

When we talk about website errors, there are two different types we need to talk about. Fatal errors cause execution of the script to halt and a page error (HTTP status code 501) to be reported to the user. An exception is an error thrown by a server-side script that may be captured through scripting and allow the web page to be displayed. An example of this kind of exception is a database query, which causes an exception but doesn't abort execution of the current script.

Building a Code Library

In order to provide consistent error handling throughout a website, a shared code module should be created that provides the majority of the error handling details. The goal here is not to repeat code so that everything is handled in one central location. That way, any changes or modifications that need to be made to the code only have to be done once. A good error handling library will contain methods for displaying a friendly message to the visitor and collecting all the debugging information needed for technical support.

Every programming language is different, so it will be up to the developer to decide how to implement the error handling. The goal should be to make it flexible and intuitive, so it can be used in many different scenarios. It should only require a minimal amount of code to wrap a section of scripting code with error handling.

Displaying Friendly Messages

There are various options for displaying friendly error messages to the user. One option is to stop processing of the entire page and display an error that reads "Sorry, this web page cannot be displayed at this time due to an internal issue. Our technical support team has been notified and will work quickly to resolve this issue." This is often the best way to handle any unexpected errors that we can handle through server-side scripting.

Another option is to display as much of the page as possible and place a highly visible error message on the screen. This message would read

"Unable to perform the action due to an internal error." The point of this type of handling is that we give the user the opportunity to correct the issue and attempt the action again. This type of situation is typically a form submission where bad data causes an error on the web page.

Debug Information

When the server-side code can handle the error, it is important that debug information is sent to the webmaster and technical support team, so issues can be resolved quickly. This debug information is different from the friendly error message displayed to the user. It contains detailed information about the code that caused the error and any other pertinent information.

One of the most common errors is a database error due to a malformed SQL statement for websites that do not use stored procedures. This type of error can easily be caught and handled through server-side code. In this case, the type of debug information we would like to see is the source of the error (file name and line number) with a stack trace and the offending SQL script that caused the error.

Some other bits of information we would like to see is the URL including the query string. The request method (GET or POST) and all form variables are passed to the script. Additionally, any cookies set on the client's machine would also be beneficial to reproduce the error. The point is, we need to get as much information as possible, so the issue can be identified and corrected quickly.

Transmitting Debug Information

Once we have this debug information, we need to transmit it to the webmaster and tech support team. The easiest way of doing this is to send an e-mail containing all the above information. Another method is to store this information in a database accessible through a company intranet.

You should consider doing both to eliminate the possibility that one method fails. Of course, if the whole script fails and stops executing, then no information will be sent out. This is one of the dangers of error handling. As a precaution to avoid this, website owners should periodically test their error handling to make sure everything works.

Webmaster Alerts

As mentioned, notifications about errors can be delivered via emai. Sometimes, it doesn't make sense to have your inbox filled with lots of e-mails. An alternative is to create an RSS Feed. RSS stands for

Really Simple Syndication or Rich Site Summary. It is like a news feed that delivers headlines along with a synopsis to users.

Using an RSS reader application, users can receive notifications through their computer or cell phone about new error reports that get generated. There are lots of code libraries available for creating RSS services on a website. It is also not too difficult to create your own custom service since an RSS feed is not much more than a dynamically-generated XML document that conforms to the RSS specification.

For even faster response times, it is fairly trivial to add a notification (or alert system) using SMS or text messaging to a cell phone number. So just like a pager was used long ago, site owners will be notified instantly whenever an issue occurs. Since it is a text message, information such as the page URL or error type can also be sent in the alert.

CONCLUSION

Python is a strong programming language that provides easy use of the code lines, great maintenance handling, and easy debugging. It has gained importance across the globe as Google has made it one of its official programming languages.

Python is a popular choice among programmers due to its simple syntax and its ease in debugging and error fixing.

Similar to many other interpretative languages, Python offers more flexibility than compiled languages, and it can be efficiently used to integrate disparate systems. Certainly, Python is a versatile programming language with several applications used in diverse fields.

Now that you have reached the end of this book, you should be able to comprehend the basics of Python and write simple lines of codes. You should also be able to comprehend the difference between the various types of data, the syntax in Python, the most important functions and modules. Although the road to become a successful programmer is still long, I hope this book will pave the path for your success, and I'm positive that, if you use the knowledge contained in it in the right way, it will definitely help you reach your goals.

Thanks for reaching the end of this book, and I hope you enjoyed it.